**Other Worlds**
and
**The Overgrown Path**

**Robert Holman**, author of **Ac... ...** and **Making Noise Quietly**, 'continues gently and unpretentiously to build himself a formidable reputation.'

Benedict Nightingale, *New Statesman*

**Other Worlds** is set in eighteenth century Yorkshire, with the threat of a French invasion hanging over the village of Fylingthorpe and nearby Robin Hood's Bay. The fishermen of the bay have long been at odds with the wealthier Fylingthorpe farmers and in this climate of feuds, ignorance and bitterness, where even the next town is peopled with enemies, the gentlest outsider becomes a target for attack.

'beautifully written'

Suzie Mackenzie, *Time Out*

**The Overgrown Path** takes place on the Greek Island of Tinos, where an ex-patriot British professor, Daniel Howarth, has been living for the last ten years with his American wife Beth. Beth was amongst the first to witness the horrors of Nagasaki in 1945. The effect of this on her, and Daniel's subsequent desire for peace, has meant a withdrawal from the world. This Greek idyll is disturbed by the arrival of a young academic and Daniel's daughter. Each discovers they have a story to tell . . .

'Slippery, insidious and finally remarkable'

Michael Coveney, *Financial Times*

**Robert Holman** was born in 1952 in Guisborough, Cleveland. He received an Arts Council Writers' Bursary in 1974 and his plays include **The Natural Cause** (Cockpit Theatre, 1974), **Mud** (Royal Court Sunday Night Production, 1974) and **Outside The Whale** (Traverse Theatre, 1976). For the Bush Theatre he has written **German Skerries** (1977), for which he was awarded the George Devine Award and **Making Noise Quietly** (1987). For the Royal Shakespeare Company he has written **Today** (1984) and **Across Oka** (1988). He has been a Resident Dramatist at the National Theatre and with the Royal Shakespeare Company in Stratford-Upon-Avon. **Other Worlds** (1983) and **The Overgrown Path** (1988) were both produced by The Royal Court. His television plays include **Chance Of A Lifetime** (BBC 1980) and **This Is History, Gran** (BBC 1986).

**Methuen New Theatrescripts** series offers frontline intelligence of the most original and exciting work from the fringe.

*authors in the same series*

Karim Alrawi
Thomas Babe
Aphra Behn
Edward Bond
Howard Brenton
Mikhail Bulgakov
Edward Bulwer-Lytton
Bob Carlton
Jim Cartwright
Caryl Churchill
Tony Craze, Ron Hart,
Johnnie Quarrell
Sarah Daniels
Nick Darke
Nick Dear
David Edgar
Harry Fierstein
Peter Flannery
Peter Gibbs
Andre Gregory
Robert Holman
Debbie Horsfield
Dusty Hughes
Ron Hutchinson
Tunde Ikoli
Terry Johnson
Charlotte Keatley
Manfred Karge
Barrie Keeffe
Paul Kember
Thomas Kilroy
Hanif Kureishi
David Lan
Deborah Levy
Kate Lock
Stephen Lowe
Doug Lucie
John Mackendrick
David Mamet

Tony Marchant
Philip Massinger
Mustapha Matura
Michael Meyer
Anthony Minghella
Adrian Mitchell
Tom Murphy
G F Newman
Louise Page
Harold Pinter
Stephen Poliakoff
Christina Reid
David Rudkin
William Saroyan
Ntozake Shange
Wallace Shawn
C P Taylor
Sue Townsend
Michelene Wandor &
Mike Alfreds
Timberlake Wertenbaker
Peter Whelan
Michael Wilcox
Nigel Williams
Snoo Wilson
Charles Wood
Nicholas Wright

# Other Worlds

# The Overgrown Path

*Two Plays by*

*Robert Holman*

**Methuen Drama**

**A Methuen New Theatrescript**

*First published in Great Britain as an original paperback in 1989 by
Methuen Drama, Michelin House, 81 Fulham Road, London SW3
6RB and distributed in the United States by HEB Inc., 70 Court
Street, Portsmouth, New Hampshire 03801. Earlier versions of* **Other
Worlds** *and* **The Overgrown Path** *were published in 1983 and
1985 respectively by Methuen Drama as part of The Royal Court
Writers series.*

*A CIP catalogue record for this book is available from the British
Library.*

ISBN 0-413-62190-1

Printed and bound in Great Britain by
Cox & Wyman Ltd, Reading

# Other Worlds

To Donald Rudd

**Other Worlds** was first performed at the Royal Court Theatre, London on 6 May 1983, with the following cast: It was directed by Richard Wilson and designed by John Byrne.

**The Fishermen**

| | |
|---|---|
| **Joe Waterman** | Paul Copley |
| **Robert Storm** | Paul Luty |
| **Molly Storm** | Anita Carey |
| **Peter Storm** | John Holmes |

**The Farmers**

| | |
|---|---|
| **Anne Wheatley** | Rosemary Leach |
| **Betsy** | Juliet Stevenson |
| **John Wheatley** | Jim Broadbent |
| **John,** *as a child* | John Holmes |
| **Richard Wheatley** | Jim Broadbent |
| **Emma Braye** | Juliet Stevenson |
| | |
| **Mary** | Lesley Dunlop |
| **Stockton** | Peter O'Farrell |
| **William Elderberry** | Peter O'Farrell |

# Scenes

*Act One*

Scene One     The beach at Bay Ness. Early Tuesday morning, July the 11th. 1797.

Scene Two     Anne Wheatley's kitchen at Middlewood Farm. An hour later.

Scene Three     Later that morning.

Scene Four     The beach and town at Robin Hood's Bay. The same morning.

*Act Two*

Scene One     Middlewood. Twenty years earlier. Mid afternoon of Christmas Eve, 1777.

Scene Two     Mid afternoon of Boxing Day.

Scene Three     The night of New Years Eve.

*Act Three*

Scene One     Anne Wheatley's kitchen. Twenty years later. The evening of July the 11th. 1797.

Scene Two     The beach and town at Robin Hood's Bay. A few moments later.

Scene Three     The beach at Bay Ness. Midday, two days later.

Intervals after Act One and Act Two.

*The play takes place near the village of Fylingthorpe and the small town of Robin Hood's Bay on the north Yorkshire coast, during the time of a threatened invasion by France.*

*Acts One and Three are set in 1797 and Act Two twenty years earlier in 1777.*

# Act One

## Scene One

*The beach at Bay Ness. Very early Tuesday morning, July the 11th. 1797.*

*The beach is empty apart from a small, rough, tent-like shelter which has been constructed from driftwood, old pieces of cloth, and canvas. Around the base of the tent seaweed has been placed to hold it down. The tent has an opening at the front, inside can be seen the figure of a child,* **Mary.**

*Darkness, almost no moon. A raging storm is blowing. A high wind. Driving rain. A wild sea is pounding violently against the shore.*

**Robert Storm** *enters from Bay Ness. He has a lantern.*

**Robert** *is a big, stocky, square, broad-shouldered man of fifty. he has a round, ruddy face which is sunburnt from his work outside, big hands, and big feet. His clothes are of poor quality; breeches, shirt, waistcoat, neck-tie, hat; no stockings and no shoes.*

**Robert** *staggers forward through the wind and rain, he is looking along the beach. He stops.*

**Robert** (*shouting over the storm*)  Is that you, Joe?

**Robert** *holds the lantern up to illuminate his face.*

**Joe Waterman** *enters from Robin Hood's Bay. He also has a lantern.*

**Joe** *is a small, thin, pinched-looking man of forty-three. His bones seem to stick through his flesh, especially on his face which is brown and sunburnt. He has a thick crop of dark hair. His clothes are of better quality; breeches, shirt, waistcoat, neck-tie, stockings, but no shoes.*

**Joe** *is blown forward with the wind. He holds the lantern to his face.*

**Joe** (*shouting, his voice not as strong as* **Robert***'s*)  Robert?

**Robert**  A've bin watchin' fo'yer.

**Robert** *walks forward. They meet.*

Yer've lost yer hat?

**Joe**  It got blown away.

**Robert** (*catching his breath*) D'know if a've sin a storm like this. It's a hundred devils were out.

**Joe** (*nodding*) Aye. What's appenin'?

**Robert** Thess a boat of Bay Ness rocks.

**Joe** *listens.*

Shiz a wreck unless we do summat. Shiz flounderin'. Lookin' f'shelter.

**Joe** (*catching his breath*) What sort of boat?

**Robert** Can't see properly. Two or three masts. A schooner. Shiz sailin' on just 'er jib.

**Joe** D'yer recognize 'er?

**Robert** (*shaking his head*) No.

*A flash of lightning.*
*They both look at the sky for a second.*

Shiz a wreck, Joe, unless we do summat.

**Joe** *nods.*

**Joe** Which way is she comin' from?

**Robert** Down the coast from Whitby.

**Joe** (*thinking*) I keep wonderin' –

**Robert** What?

**Joe** She might be a French boat.

*A loud clap of thunder.*
*They look at the sky and wait for it to finish.*

**Robert** You know best, Joe.

**Joe** It's jus' the sort a'night the French would come. A night like this. Tryin' to catch us out. When we're not expectin' 'em.

**Robert** *looks perplexed.*
**Mary** *comes out of her shelter.*

**Mary** *is a small, thin girl of about fourteen, though she looks and is dressed like a boy. Her hair is roughly cut and her skin is ingrained with months of dirt. Her clothes are ill-fitting and ragged: trousers, shirt, waistcoat, jacket, a cap on her head; no stockings and no shoes.*

**Mary** *staggers forward towards* **Robert** *and* **Joe.**

A don' know what t'do. Are the beacons ready?

**Robert** (*nodding*)  Yeh.

**Robert**'s *hat nearly blows off, he pulls it back on.*
**Mary** *is beside them.*

**Mary**  What yer doin' 'ere?

**Robert** (*gruffly*)  Thess a boat in trouble, boy.

**Joe**  If we light the beacons does she stan' a chance?

**Robert**  More'n she do now.

**Joe** (*shouting more loudly*)  A wish a could be sure it weren't the French. (*After thinking for a moment*) Alright, light 'em. We'll tekk the risk.

**Robert** *walks a pace or two towards Bay Ness. He waves his lantern from side to side.*
**Joe** *and* **Mary** *watch.*

**Mary** (*pointing, excited*)  Look, there the' go. I ain't seen tha' before, Master.

*A flash of lightning.* **Mary** *covers her head with her hands.* **Robert** *stops waving the lantern.* **Joe** *walks to him.*

**Joe**  I hope it's not the French army?

**Robert**  Aye. Are yer comin' or a'yer goyn back?

**Joe**  I'll come with yer.

**Robert**  We'll go then.

**Robert** *and* **Joe** *walk towards Bay Ness.*

**Mary**  Where yer goyn? Can I come?

**Robert** *and* **Joe** *have exited.*
*A loud clap of thunder.* **Mary** *covers her head with her hands.*

Why can't a come? Yer all the same you fishermen.

*The moonlight fades to blackout.*
*The sound of the storm remains.*

Scene Two

**Anne Wheatley**'s *kitchen at Middlewood Farm. An hour later.*

*The kitchen is quite small and has a stone floor. The walls have been roughly plastered and whitewashed. In the back wall there is a sash window which is set in a small recess. When it is light an oak tree can be seen growing outside. At the base of the window, set in the recess, is a rough oak ledge which serves as a kitchen work surface. In front of the window is an oak table and a wooden bench. Beside the window, to the left, is the outside door. The door is secured from the inside by a bar of wood; at the moment the bar is resting against the wooden door frame. In the left-hand wall is a brick oven, the chimney-breast leads upwards from it. The oven is newer than the rest of the kitchen, it was built ten years ago. On the chimney-breast are two wooden shelves. Standing against the right-hand wall is a fine oak dresser. Down-stage of the dresser is a door leading to the rest of the house, and upstairs. Near the dresser is a rocking-chair.*

**Anne** *keeps her kitchen clean and tidy. On the ledge below the window are various cooking items; a sugar loaf; various dried herbs, some hanging free, some in small wooden boxes; a copper jelly mould; an iron toast-rack; a wooden butter-pat; wooden and iron spoons, copper ladels, etc. Leaning against the oven is a pair of firetongs. Above the oven on the two ledges are cooking-pots, skillets, saucepans of various sizes, the bigger ones are made of iron and the smaller ones of copper. Standing on the oven is a kettle and a toasting fork. The dresser is decorated with china and pewter plates, wine glasses and goblets. Dotted throughout the kitchen are candles and rushlights in holders. On the table, covered by a muslin cloth, are various cooked meats, bread and pies.*

*A faint moonlight through the window.*

*The storm is still raging, though now the scene being inside, it is muffled.*

**Mary** *appears outside at the window.*

*A flash of lightning.*

**Mary** *covers her head with her hands for a moment. She tries the window, it opens. She lifts it up and clambers in. In doing so she knocks various items off the window ledge, they clatter to the floor.*

*Thunder outside.*

**Mary** *closes the window. She looks about the kitchen, peering into*

*things. Eventually she lifts the muslin cloth on the table and sees the*
*food. She picks up a meat pie and starts to eat it. She is starving; bits*
*of pie drop onto the floor.* **Mary** *has a canvas bag with her, while she*
*is eating she packs the bag with the rest of the food. Suddenly she stops.*
*She has heard someone upstairs, she goes to the window and tries to*
*open it. The window is stuck.* **Mary** *hides under the window ledge.*

*The door to the rest of the house opens.* **Anne Wheatley** *peers round,*
*she has a candle.*

**Anne** *is a plump woman of fifty nine. She has a gentle, intelligent,*
*homely face and her hair has gone grey. Her hands and fingers are*
*slightly red with rheumatism. She is wearing a white nightdress and a*
*woollen shawl.*

**Anne** *steps gingerly into the kitchen. In her other hand she has an iron*
*poker.*

*She is followed in by* **Betsy**. **Betsy** *has a candle in one hand and a*
*broom handle in the other, she looks frightened.*

**Betsy** *is a slim, attractive girl of nineteen. She is taller than* **Anne**,
*and has a clean, bright, alert face, and short blond hair. She is*
*wearing a white nightdress.*

*The kitchen has brightened with the candlelight.*

**Betsy**  See anyone?

**Anne**  You've gone white, girl.

**Betsy**  I don't think I heard anything after all, Aunt.

**Anne**  Close the door.

**Betsy** *nervously closes the door.*

(*Bravely and quite gently*)  Stay by it.

**Betsy** (*staying by the door*)  Please, Aunt, it must've been the
storm.

**Anne** (*walking to the table*)  Look at this. There is someone in
here.

**Betsy**  I hope he's escaped.

**Anne** (*walking to the outside door*)  The door's unbolted.

**Betsy**  I heard Master John go out.

**Anne** *puts the wooden bar across the door.*

**Anne**  You've done very little sleeping, have you, girl?

*A flash of lightning.*
**Betsy** *jumps. They both look towards the window.*

I've never seen such a night, Now, where is this thief? You didn't hear him go out?

**Betsy**  No.

*Thunder outside.*
**Betsy** *jumps.* **Anne** *starts to search the kitchen, looking under and over things.*

(*Nervously*) I know who it is.

**Anne**  Who?

**Betsy**  Appleyard's lad.

**Anne**  Tim Appleyard?

**Betsy**  I've seen him hiding in the trees, he's bin watching us.

**Anne** (*raising her voice*) Come out Tim Appleyard, if you're in here, we know it's you.

**Mary** *tries to push herself further under the window.*

**Betsy** (*raising her voice*) I've seen you, Tim Appleyard.

**Anne** *puts the candle on the table. She holds the poker in both hands and searches the kitchen again.*

Be careful, he's a big lad.

**Anne**  I've some puff in me still.

**Betsy** (*calling*) Did you hear that, Appleyard's boy?

**Anne** *looks by the dresser.*

**Anne**  A good-for-nothing since the day of his birth, that's Tim Appleyard.

**Betsy**  I'm glad your poker's brave.

**Anne**  Don't prattle, Betsy.

**Mary** *comes out.*

**Betsy** (*screaming*) Aunt! There 'e is!

**Mary** *climbs onto the window ledge.*

**Anne** I've got 'im.

**Mary** *tries to open the window. Before she can succeed* **Anne** *has got to her.* **Anne** *hits out at* **Mary** *with the poker. The blows are quite hard across* **Mary**'s *back.*

**Betsy** (*shrieking*) You've done it, you've done it! You've got 'im, you've got 'im!

**Mary** *falls off the window ledge onto the floor, she rolls up into a ball.* **Anne** *continues to hit out.*

**Betsy** *goes to the table and puts her candle down.*
**Anne**'s *blows slowly cease. She stops.*

**Anne** (*out of breath*) He's had enough now.

**Anne** *looks dishevelled, her hair has fallen out of place, and her shawl has fallen on the floor. She picks it up and puts it back across her shoulders. She is breathing deeply.*

**Betsy** Are you all right?

**Anne** (*walking to the rocking-chair*) I haven't as much puff as I thought.

**Anne** *sits in the rocking-chair.*

I'll be all right in a minute.

*A slight pause.*

**Betsy** You hit him quit hard.

**Anne** Yes.

*A slight pause.* **Betsy** *looks at* **Mary.**

**Betsy** It's not Tim Appleyard.

**Anne** No.

**Betsy** I've never seen 'im before. I don't know who 'e is, d'you?

**Anne** No, child.

**Betsy** He's just a child 'imself. (*Still concerned about* **Anne.**) You were brave.

**Anne** *is breathing more easily, she stands up and walks back towards* **Mary.**

**Anne** We'd best find out who he is.

**Betsy**  He hasn't moved. You don' think he's dead?

**Anne**  He's breathing thank goodness.

**Betsy**  Yes.

**Anne**  I let my arm take over. Let it be a lesson f'you.

*A flash of lightning.*
**Betsy** *jumps.*

**Betsy**  I wish the lightning'd stop.

**Anne**  What is your name, child?

*A slight pause.*

Tell me where you've come from?

*A slight pause.*

**Betsy**  Nowhere, Aunt.

**Anne**  You're not from Flyingthorpe or the farms round about, are you? (*After a moment's pause. Looking up at* **Betsy**.) He's not a fisherman, I hope?

**Betsy** (*worry in her voice*)  How could he be?

**Anne**  It's a silly thought.

**Betsy** (*to* **Mary**)  We don't talk to the fishermen.

**Anne**  You're not a fisherman from Robin Hood's Bay, are you?

*A slight pause.*

**Betsy**  He's not, Aunt.

**Anne**  I don't know what to think. (*To* **Mary**.) Tell me your name, child, and I won't hurt you more.

**Mary** *is still silent.*

**Betsy** (*picking up* **Mary**'s *canvas bag*)  He must've been hungry.

**Betsy** *puts the bag on the table and starts to unpack the food* **Mary** *has taken.*

All he's taken is the food.

**Anne** (*after a moment's pause*)  What am I going to do with him, Betsy?

**Anne** *bends down and takes hold of* **Mary**'*s shoulders.*

Stand up, child, let's see you more clearly.

**Mary** (*wriggling, shouting*)  Ge' off me.

**Anne**  But you can't stay there all night.

**Anne** *lets* **Mary** *go.* **Betsy** *has put the food on the table.*

**Betsy**  He's eaten one pie.

**Anne** (*taking* **Mary**'*s shoulders again*)  Stand up, come on.

**Mary** (*wriggling, shouting*)  No.

**Anne** *tries to lift* **Mary** *up.* **Mary** *kicks out with her feet.*

Ge' off! Stop it!

**Anne**  You're going to stand up.

**Betsy**  Be careful, Aunt, he's kicking.

**Anne**  I know where he's kicking, he's going to do as he's told.

**Mary**  Ge' off me!

**Anne** (*smacking* **Mary**'*s bottom*)  Stop it.

**Mary** *stops struggling, she stands up.* **Anne**'*s hair has fallen out of place.*

Now then, that's better.

**Mary** *spits at* **Anne.**

I'm doing you a kindness, child. (*Pushing her hair back.*) For such a little mite you're very strong.

**Mary** *spits at* **Anne.**
*Thunder outside.*

Thunder outside an' thunder in here. Would you pick those things up off the floor, Betsy.

**Betsy** *goes to the window. She starts to pick up the things* **Mary** *knocked off and return them to the ledge.*

**Mary**  This is my kitchen.

**Anne**  It is, is it?

**Mary**  Well it ain't yours. Yer hurt me.

**Betsy**  I think he must be living wild, Aunt.

**Mary**  (*aggressively to* **Betsy**)  'Ow would you know?

**Anne**  (*to* **Mary**)  Let's have no more.

**Mary**  Who's she?

**Anne**  (*quite gently*)  Betsy is my niece.

**Mary**  Bit funny, ain't she?

**Betsy**  Not as funny as you.

**Anne**  Would both of you cease. (*After a moment's pause.*) I want the boy to talk, Betsy.

**Mary**  I ain' a thief, Mistress.

**Anne**  Then why are you in my kitchen?

**Mary**  Cos – cos I'm 'ungry.

**Anne**  When did you last eat something?

**Mary**  (*pointing at it*)  That pie. All I've 'ad f'days'n days.

**Anne**  And are you living wild as my neice said?

**Mary**  On the beach, Mistress.

**Anne**  With the fishermen?

**Mary** *is silent.*

With the fishermen, child?

**Mary**  (*not sure what to say*)  Aye. A like them lot.

**Betsy** *stands up and listens.*

**Anne**  Have they talked to you?

**Mary**  (*looking between* **Anne** *and* **Betsy**)  All the time, Mistress. The' give me food.

**Anne**  Then why are you starving now?

**Mary**  D'know.

**Anne**  (*after a moment's pause*)  Did the fishermen send you here?

**Mary**  Yeh, the' did.

**Anne**  (*after a moment's pause*)  Why did they send you?

**Mary**  D'know, Mistress. The didn't.

**Betsy** *starts to pick up the last of the things off the floor.*

**Anne**  How long've you been like this, child?

**Mary**  Weeks'n weeks. Months.

**Betsy** (*standing up*)  I've picked those up.

**Anne**  Thank you, Betsy.

**Betsy**  D'you think he is with the fishermen?

**Anne**  I'm sure not.

**Mary** (*looking at* **Anne**)  What yer goyn t'do wi' me?

**Anne**  I don't know.

**Betsy**  He doesn't seem very old t'me.

**Anne**  How old are you?

**Mary** *shrugs.*

**Mary**  Can' count, Mistress. 'Bout thirty two, summat like.

**Anne**  My son's thirty two. He's a man.

**Mary**  'Bout eighteen then.

**Anne** (*gently*)  Sit down.

**Mary** *sits down on the bench.* **Anne** *walks to the rocking-chair and sits down.*

If you're not from Bay Town where are you from?

**Mary** *shrugs.*

Don't you know that either?

**Mary**  Stockton.

**Anne**  Whereabouts is Stockton, child?

**Mary** (*pointing*)  That way.

**Betsy**  Shuvv up, boy.

**Mary** *moves along.* **Betsy** *sits down on the bench.*

**Mary**  A've bin walkin' a lot.

**Anne**  'N' what's your name?

**Mary**  The call me Jack. Skip-Jack. Cos I used t'skip all the time.

*The storm is slowly beginning to blow itself out and quieten.*

Where abouts am a?

**Anne**  You're near the village of Fylingthorpe on the North Yorkshire coast.

**Mary**  Is this a farm?

**Anne**  (*brightly*)  My son John runs the farm.

**Mary**  'Ave you any cows?

**Anne**  Three.

**Mary**  A can milk cows. 'Ave you a job, Mistress?

**Anne**  I don't think so, child.

**Mary**  A can milk cows till me fingers drop off. A c'd live in the barn.

**Betsy**  (*shivering*)  I'm cold.

**Mary**  A've slept wi' pigs, a c'd live wi' them?

**Anne**  My son decides such things.

**Mary**  Only want a home.

**Anne**  I expect you do, child, but how can I have you?

**Mary**  Oh please, please.

**Betsy**  He's some politeness about 'im now.

**Mary**  A'd eat the pigs food.

**Betsy**  I'm cold, Aunt, why don't we let 'im go?

**Anne** *thinks.*

It's not as if he's Appleyard's lad, we won't see 'im again.

**Anne**  I don't want him at Bay Town, Betsy.

**Betsy**  It don't matter, do it?

**Anne**  (*heartfelt*)  How I wish it didn't very of'en.

**Mary**  This is my home now, ain' it?

**Anne**  We don't know anything about you, you can't stay here.

**Anne** *is thinking*.

**Betsy**  I'll be bold, Aunt, I think you're being silly.

**Anne**  Choose your words with care.

**Betsy**  I'm sorry.

**Anne** *thinks for a moment longer and then looks at the window*.

**Anne** (*brightly*)  Thank the Lord the storm is ceasing.

**Betsy**  It seems t'be.

**Anne** (*leaning forward*)  If I let you go, boy, will you run away and not go back to the fishermen?

**Mary** *shrugs*.

We had a feud with Bay Town many years ago.

**Betsy** (*to* **Mary**)  They stink you know, with the smell of fish. One fisherman has two heads.

**Anne** (*standing up*)  Who on this earth told you that?

**Betsy**  Stephen Cleese at 'Thorpe village.

**Anne**  Such tales belong in books.

**Betsy**  He had a pipe in one mouth an' was eating with the other.

**Anne** (*turning, walking to the dresser*)  Gossip, Betsy. The villagers only make things worse.

**Betsy**  The villagers believe him, Aunt.

**Anne**  I expect they do in their foolishness. Is that reason f'us to?

**Betsy**  No.

**Anne** *picks up a small wooden box from the dresser, it contains yarrow leaves*.

**Anne** (*putting some leaves into a small bowl*)  Stephen Cheese was not alive those twenty years ago. He's never been to Bay.

**Anne** *adds a few drops of water to the bowl from the kettle by the fire*.

**Betsy**  The villagers believe him because it was he who saw the soldiers comin'. (*To* **Mary**)  The press gang came here.

**Mary** *looks blank.*

Don't you know about the war?

**Anne** *has found a wooden spoon, she is mixing a paste with the yarrow leaves and water. She sits down.*

We're at war with France. A platoon of soldiers arrived here in their gleaming blue uniforms an' took away those that didn't hide quick enough.

**Anne** Don't exaggerate f'the boy. Some men wanted t'go, child.

**Betsy** Only the faggers, Aunt, the poor. Only those fit for nothing else.

**Anne** (*leaning back in the chair*) I tire of your prattle.

**Anne** *closes her eyes.*

The poor deserve our respect. What else could they do?

**Betsy** (*subdued*) I know we're lucky, Aunt, I didn't mean it that way.

*A slight pause.*

I do respect the poor. I thank the Lord everynight in my prayers.

**Anne** *opens her eyes.* **Mary** *scratches her aching back.*

Why doesn't the lad go in the army?

**Anne** D'you really not know about the war?

**Mary** *shakes her head*

The army is a good life for a boy your age. The faggers, their lads went, all boys like you. They're fighting France.

**Mary** (*scratching her back*) Soldiers chased me once. At the market town of Guisborough. A ran off.

**Anne** Does your back sting?

**Mary** *nods.*

Come here, child, and I'll rub some yarrow leaves on it.

**Mary** No.

**Anne** The yarrow leaves will help soothe it. (*Standing up.*) Stand up'n take your shirt off.

**Mary** (*hesitantly standing up*) No, a don' wan' it.

**Anne** (*walking to* **Mary**) What's the matter with you now?

**Mary** (*walking away a step*) Ge'off me. Leave me alone.

**Anne** (*gently*) All right child.

**Betsy** The boy doesn't want to be naked in front of two women.

*There is a loud knock at the outside door.*

**Anne** Who's that?

**Betsy** It'll be Master John come back.

**Anne** *puts the wooden bowl on the table and goes to the door.*

**Anne** Is that you, John?

**John** (*from outside*) What's going on?

**Anne** Wait a minute, I bolted the door.

**Anne** *removes the wooden bar and rests it against the door frame.*

*The door opens.* **John Wheatley** *enters, he is soaking wet.*

**John** *is a tall, broad-shouldered man of thirty-two. He has rough hands, thick dark hair, and a sunburnt face. His clothes are of good quality; shoes, stockings, breeches, silk shirt, waistcoat, jacket, neck-tie, and a hat.*

**John** (*closing the door, taking his hat off*) I saw the candlelight, now the door, what's going on?

**John** *turns and sees* **Mary**.

Who's that?

**Anne** He broke into our kitchen.

**John** *puts his hat on the table and walks towards* **Mary**. **Mary** *backs away.*

**Betsy** (*her voice rising*) Don't Master John, he's had a sound thrashing from the Mistress here.

**John** *stops.*

**John** (*looking at his mother*)  Ma?

**Anne**  Betsy spoke the truth.

**John** (*looking at* **Mary**)  What does the boy say?

**Mary** *is silent*.

(*Going to* **Mary**)  I'll lock him with the hens.

**Anne**  Then what?

**John** (*taking* **Mary** *roughly by the arm*)  Take him to the Justice in Whitby when it's light.

**Mary** *kicks* **John.**

He kicked me.

**John** *increases his hold on* **Mary.**

**Anne**  Would you go to bed please, Betsy.

**John**  I'm not having a row, Ma.

**Anne**  Yes, you are.

**Betsy** *walks to the upstairs door*.

**Mary** (*trying to kick* **John** *again*)  Ge' off me.

**John**  Don't you go.

**Betsy**  This time I agree with the Mistress. Goodnight.

**Anne**  Goodnight, Betsy.

**Betsy** *exits upstairs and closes the door*.

**Mary** *is struggling*.

Will you let the boy go.

**Mary** *stops struggling*.

I shouldn't have to ask you again.

*A slight pause*.

Will you let the boy go please.

**John** *lets* **Mary** *go*. **Mary** *struggles free of his hands*.

(*to* **Mary**)  Come here.

**Mary**, *a little bewildered, walks to* **Anne**.

He's spending the rest of the night in here. If in the morning you still want to take him to the Justice, that's up to you.

**John** (*his voice rising*)  I haven't done anything. What've I done? Tell me, Ma?

**Anne**  I'm tired, John.

**John** *looks down for a moment.*

**John** (*looking up, calmly*)  I come back, there's a boy in the kitchen who's a thief, what am I expected t'do?

**Anne**  I'm not only talking about now.

**John**  What are yer talkin' about?

**Anne**  Wilf Meadows, yesterday morning. I saw you shouting at him in that terrible manner. I felt ashamed.

**John**  Wilf Meadows is our shepherd. He'd lost five sheep.

**Anne**  But you found them again.

**John**  I found 'em. In Middlewood. Is that what this is all about?

**Anne**  Only partly, John.

**John**  Yer find funny ways of goyn about it. What else?

**Anne**  I've tried to say – your manner and your bullying.

**John** *takes his pocket watch from his waistcoat pocket.*

**John**  It's four o'clock in the morning.

**John** *puts the watch away.*

*The storm is now much quieter, it has almost blown itself out.*

**Anne**  Where've you been?

**John**  I couldn't sleep. I wen' out to look at the farm.

**Anne** (*to* **Mary**)  Sit in the chair.

**Mary** *walks to the rocking-chair and sits down.*

Is the farm in a mess?

**John** (*walking to the bench, sitting down*)  Most of the wheat is down.

**Anne** (*walking to the bench, sitting down beside him*) Will the faggers be able to cut it?

**John** It'd begun to ripen, Ma. It's now as flat as the mill pond. Five Acre was yellow with ripening.

**Anne** *looks tenderly at* **John.**

(*Slightly more brightly*) Aye it'll cut if it don't rot first. A harder job f'the faggers, that's all.

**Anne** *smiles.*

At least yer smilin' now. Yer won't be when a tell yer this. Lightning struck one o' your cows.

**Anne** Which one?

**John** Celandine. The silly beast got 'ersel' beneath the oak tree in Bottom Meadow.

**Anne** Is she dead?

**John** Aye, she is. I'm sorry, Ma. The trees down an' all. A were fond of that oak tree.

**Anne** So was I.

**John** (*tenderly*) Celandine was your favourite, wasn't she?

**Anne** She'd the best disposition.

**John** Will you buy another cow?

**Anne** I'd like to, John. Her milk was always best for the butter, too.

**John** Aye, well, we'll do that. (*Smiling.*) I'll grumble till I'm sick about the money.

**Anne** I'm sorry if I sometimes seem harsh.

**John** Yer do'n all. 'N' why send Betsy t'bed?

**Anne** *smiles.*

I know why an' that smile proves it. T'get yer own way.

**Anne** I haven't yet, have I?

**John** (*less tenderly*) No, an' we'll see if yer do.

*Silence for a moment.*

**Anne** (*turning, looking at the window*)  The storm has stopped, thank goodness.

**John** (*standing, walking to the oven*)  I went up t'Bay Ness.

**Anne**  What on earth for?

**John** (*holding his hands above the oven*)  The fishermen were on the beach, tryin' t'save a boat.

**Anne**  Did they?

**John**  No, it was wrecked.

**Anne**  I hope God has mercy upon them.

**John**  By the time the' lit the beacons the boat didn' stand a chance. (*Gingerly touching the top of the oven.*) The oven's not in.

**John** *touches the oven with the palm of his hand.*

**Anne**  I was going to re-light it at dawn. Why did you go to Bay Ness?

**John** (*turning to face* **Anne**)  I don't trust 'em, Ma. If the French do come, it'll be a night like this. 'N' if they're not watching –

**Anne**  I think they will watch, John.

**John**  Yer've faith f'a dozen. Farmer Wood had the same idea. I met him there.

**Anne** *pulls a face.*

The strong wind'd blown the thatch from 'is barn. All his hay inside.

**Anne**  Farmer Wood is an idle drunkard.

**John**  It's no wonder 'e don't like you.

**Anne**  I wouldn't expect to be liked by any of the Wood family. They're all as idle as a stopped clock.

**John**  I think yer do it on purpose.

**Anne** (*huffily*)  What?

**John**  Everyone talks about yer, Ma.

**Anne**  Do they. Let them. It's gossip with no meaning.

**John**  They've started to say yer a witch.

**Anne** Who're they?

**John** The villagers at 'Thorpe.

**Anne** Bring those villagers to me. I speak my mind. Always have done. I won't change now. I'm not on God's earth to be loved by the villagers of 'Thorpe. And I hope you defend me, John?

*A slight pause.*

Do you defend me?

*A slight pause.*

Obviously you don't.

**John** I try to, Ma.

**Anne** (*after a moment's pause, calmly*) Witch is a very strong word.

**John** I know that.

**Anne** I'll have to go t'the village.

*The first faint light of dawn can be seen through the window.*

(*Standing.*) It's beginning to get light.

**John** I've to muck out the pigs. Sally is lookin' restless, 'er litters near due.

**Anne** *walks to* **Mary**.

'N' I'll bring up Celandine from the meadow. We'll have some beef, all be it a bit tough, she was an old lass.

**Anne** Have you decided about the boy? The Justice will have him whipped from one end of the village to the other.

**John** (*his voice rising*) If he's with a band of sheep stealers, Ma.

**Anne** He's not.

**John** *thinks for a moment.*

**John** A whipping is no less than he deserves.

**Mary** I've bin whipped before. At the market town of Guisborough. A put some paper down me breeches.

**John**  D'you promise me t'run away? Somewhere else 'n' never come back.

**Anne**  The boy will run. He's been running. He's used to running.

*A slight pause.*

**John**  Alright, Ma, but this is the last time. (*Walking to the upstairs door.*) I'll go upstairs 'n' change these wet clothes.

**Anne**  I'll make breakfast, John.

**John**  It's against my better judgement.

**John** *exits through the upstairs door and closes it behind him.*

**Anne** *goes to the table and starts to pack the canvas bag with the food.*

**Anne**  Think yourself lucky, child.

**Mary** (*standing up*)  Wha'?

**Mary** *walks to* **Anne**.

**Anne**  Run away. And never come back as the Master said.

**Mary**  A don' want t'.

**Anne**  Don't be silly. (*Putting the bag over* **Mary**'s *shoulder.*) I can't help you.

**Anne** *pushes* **Mary** *towards the outside door.*

**Mary**  Why can't a stay?

**Anne** *opens the door.*

**Anne**  Go on run, child, run.

**Mary** (*staying put*)  Where am a runnin' to?

**Anne**  Away from here. Run, go on, run.

**Mary** *runs through the door.*

As fast as your legs will carry you.

*A slight pause.*

That's it.

**Anne** *stands watching through the open door.*
*In the dawn light the two candles are still burning.*

Scene Three

**Anne Wheatley's** *kitchen. Later that morning.*

*The sash window and the outside door are open.*

*Sunlight is streaming in. It is a bright, warm, sunny day.*

*On the table is a plate of sweet pig meat, some butter in a dish, and a milk jug.*

*A song thrush sings outside.*

**Betsy** *enters through the open door, in one hand she is carrying a wooden pail which is half full of water, and in the other she is clutching four big apples, an onion, and a carrot. She is wearing shoes, a gown, an apron, and a cap on her head.*

**Betsy** *puts the pail down near the table. The apples, onion, and carrot she puts near the pig meat. Next she starts to find, and bring to the table, all the things she will need to make a pie: bowls, spoons, etc. She lays them out ready. When she has finished she looks at the table for a moment.*

**Betsy** *goes to the upstairs door and opens it.*

**Betsy** (*calling through*) Mistress, are you back yet?

*No answer.* **Betsy** *walks to the outside door and looks out for a moment.*
*The song thrush sings again.*
**Betsy** *goes to the dresser and takes a broken china cup from the top ledge. She takes a key from the cup, bends down, and opens one of the cupboards at the bottom of the dresser. From the back of the cupboard she takes a notebook, (it is* **Anne**'s *diary), she goes to the table, clears a space, and sits down to read. She turns the page, reading with great interest.*

**John** *appears at the outside door. He is wearing shoes, stockings, breeches, shirt, neck-tie, and a hat. His hands and clothes are covered in pig muck.* **John** *watches* **Betsy** *for a moment.*

**John** Betsy.

**Betsy** (*jumping out of her skin*) Oh, Master John, you gave me a shock. Don't do that. (*Trying to hide the notebook.*) What's happened t'yer?

**John** I've fell in the pig muck.

**Betsy** *smiles and stands up.*

Don't you dare laugh.

**Betsy** *smirks and trys not to laugh.*

(*Severely*)  Betsy.

**Betsy**  Don't you come in here for goodness sake, the Mistress will have a blue fit. (*Almost laughing.*) If you could see yourself.

**John**  That stupid sow, Sally, knocked me right over.

**Betsy** *sniffs.*

**Betsy**  I can stink you from here, Master John. Go'n rub yourself with parsley, that'll help rid of it. (*Laughing.*) Otherwise yer'll stink f'weeks.

**John** (*walking into the kitchen*)  If I'm going' to suffer, you will.

**Betsy** (*trying to be firm, but laughing*)  No, Master John, don't be annoyin'. If the Mistress –

**John**  I'm the head of the house, Betsy. (*Sitting down on the bench.*) Make me a cup of tea. (*Seing the notebook.*) What're you doin'?

**Betsy** (*huffily*)  Nothin'.

**John** (*pulling the notebook towards him*)  This is the Mistress's diary.

**Betsy**  I know.

**John**  Reading it again? One day, she'll catch you.

**Betsy**  She won't, I only read it when she's not here.

**John**  Don't look t'me if she does.

**Betsy**  She's gone t'Thorpe, t'see Appleyard's wife about our washin' next week.

**John**  Has it never occurred t'yer that she might know?

**Betsy**  What?

**John**  She might know yer read her diary.

**Betsy** (*taking the notebook from* **John**)  Of course she don't.

**John**  The Mistress is cleverer than that.

**Betsy** *closes the notebook.*

She don't do much that's not on purpose.

**Betsy** *walks with the notebook to the dresser.*

Where's this tea yer mekkin' me?

**Betsy** I can stink yer, Master John.

**Betsy** *puts the notebook back in the cupboard.*

**John** Why didn't you support me las' night?

**Betsy** (*locking the cupboard*) I was tired.

**John** Tell me why the Mistress crosses me?

**Betsy** (*putting the key in the cup*) Your bad temper, I should think.

**Betsy** *replaces the cup on the dresser.*

(*Walking back to the table*) I've to busy myself. Where's the knife.

*A knife is not on the table, she finds one on the window ledge.*

**John** Why doesn't she like me, Betsy?

**Betsy** Such nonsense I've never heard. (*Starting to cut the pig meat into cubes.*) You are right in my way, Master John.

**John** *moves out of her way towards* **Anne**'s *chair.*

Do you like the Mistress?

**John** She's my mother.

**Betsy** If you don't like her, how can she like you?

**John** (*angrily*) I'm head of the house.

**John** *sits.*

Why don't folk like me, Betsy? Thess only David Wood an' 'e's a drunkard according to my mother.

**Betsy** He is a drunkard, the Mistress is right.

**John** Even you think so.

*A slight pause.*

All the village girls spurn me.

**Betsy** Would you like to take a wife, Master John? The Mistress would like you to wed. She worries about you.

**John** (*heartfelt*) I worry too.

*A slight pause.*

**Betsy** A girl likes to be courted gently. Be given some flowers from the field, 'n' treated fair. (*Her face breaking into a smile.*) Not wooed by a silly pig man with shite all over 'im. (*Putting down the knife, laughing.*) I'm sorry, I can't help it, you're so funny sometimes.

**John** (*gritting his teeth*) I can keep my temper.

**Betsy** I'll have to look the other way.

**Betsy** *looks away from* **John**, *she picks up the knife and continues to cut the meat. She stops laughing.*

**John** Finished with your fun?

**Betsy** *nods, holding back the laugh.*

I've a temper, have I?

**Betsy** You know you have, Master John.

**John** I've my father's temper. It will go, it will vanish like a morning mist.

*A slight pause.*

And when it's gone completely, which may take a few weeks, my mother will do exactly as I say. As will you.

**Betsy** *nods.*

There'll be no more thieving boys set free from this kitchen.

*A slight pause.*

No longer will the folk of 'Thorpe say I sleep in my mother's bed. Nor say my mother's a witch.

**Betsy** *holds back another laugh. She has finished cutting the meat, she starts to peel the four apples with the knife.*

I'll go to the village, t'the New Plough Inn. Give ol' Chris Smith twopence t'play his fiddle. 'N' I'll dance, mighty jollily, with all the girls. I'll be the gossip of 'Thorpe for my changed manner.

*A slight pause.*

I'll sow hemp seed beside Harriet Woodforde's door, because

she's the girl of my fancy. We'll be married within eighteen months.

**Betsy**   I should tell 'er first, Master John.

**John**   *holds his temper.*

**John**   I won't have to force her to kiss me anymore. Or get her drunk which costs money. Or get drunk myself.

*A slight pause.*

(*Happily.*)   What're you makin'?

**Betsy**   A pig meat pie.

**John**   F'dinner?

**Betsy**   (*still holding back the laugh*)   Yes.

**John**   Yer a fine cook.

**Betsy**   Thank you, I do my best.

**John**   (*standing up*)   Don't turn against me, Betsy. My father was never disobeyed.

**Betsy**   I didn't know 'im, did I. I was four when he had his riding accident, and died.

**John**   (*wiping the chair clean*)   He was a fine'n strong man. With the intelligence of an Eagle. He would have had the boy whipped.

**Betsy**   *nods slightly.*

I loved my father. Never believe what my mother sez.

**John**   *walks to the window and looks out.*

**Betsy**   She never talks about 'im, Master John. But if your father had had that boy whipped he would've been cruel.

**John**   Wilf Meadow's arrived back from the moor. He's two sheep with him. I won't have time for tea.

**John**   *walks towards the door.*   **Betsy**   *stops peeling the apples.*

**Betsy**   Master John.

**John**   *stops and turns.*

The Mistress loves you more than you know. Just as she loves me. 'N' if she does know I read her diarys, it's because she wants me to. Your father was a cruel man. She's lived the years since his death brooding on it.

**John**  You've a foul tongue, Betsy. (*Viciously.*) One day someone will cut it out.

**John** *turns and exits through the open door.*

*After a moment* **Betsy** *picks up the knife and continues to peel the apples. The song thrust sings. A slight pause.*

**Anne** *enters through the outside door. She is wearing shoes, a gown, a red cloak, and a bonnet. Her shoes and the bottom of her gown are muddy.*

**Anne**  John's jus' sped past me in a ferocious mood.

**Betsy**  He fell in some pig shite, Aunt.

**Anne**  Is that what it was. (*Taking off her cloak.*) I can cope with his temper, it's a bright sunny day. The path to the village is muddy after all the rain. (*Putting the cloak over her arm.*) You have got on well.

**Betsy**  Daisy and Hawthorn didn't give much milk.

**Anne** (*taking off her bonnet*)  I wouldn't expect them to. (*Walking to the upstairs door.*) The lightning scares them and drys them up.

**Betsy**  They must be missing Celandine. Did you see Appleyard's wife?

**Anne**  She's coming on Tuesday f'the washing, a week today. (*Opening the door.*) She'll sleep the night here. That way we'll make an early start.

**Anne** *goes out.*

**Betsy** *finishes peeling the apples, she walks to the dresser, finds a wooden bowl and brings it back to the table. She starts to core the apples and cut them up into the bowl.*
*The song thrush sings.*
**Betsy** *whistles, imitating it.*
**Anne** *returns minus the cloak and bonnet. She sniffs.*

The stink is still here.

**Anne** *goes to the dresser and opens another cupboard at the bottom. The key is already in the lock.*

Tim Appleyard is a bad sort.

**Betsy** Did you challenge 'im about hidin' in the woods?

**Anne** (*taking an apron and a cap from the cupboard*) I did. He told me some terrible lies.

**Betsy** What lies?

**Anne** (*closing the cupboard door*) All in front of his mother as well. (*Standing up.*) His mother scolded him roundly.

**Anne** *starts to put the apron on.*

**Betsy** What lies, Aunt?

**Anne** I'm not sure I should say, they were so terrible. Appleyard's wife is a grand sort, it's not fair.

**Anne** *starts to put the cap on.*

He's an eye for you, that's what it amounts to.

**Betsy** Tim Appleyard has?

**Anne** A big and roving eye.

**Betsy** What did he say?

**Anne** He said he's been watching you.

**Betsy** Me? (*Suspiciously.*) What for?

**Anne** As I say the lies are terrible.

**Betsy** (*looking at* **Anne**) Tell me truthfully, Aunt?

**Anne** (*looking at* **Betsy**) Well, Tim Appleyard said he's been following you through Middlewood, towards Bay Town.

**Betsy** 'E said that?

**Anne** Indeed he did, child. An' that in Middlewood you meet a fisherman, and there you make passionate love to one another.

**Betsy** I don't believe it.

**Anne** He's been roundly scolded. It's not so, is it?

**Betsy** Of course not, Aunt.

**Anne** Then I want to hear no more.

**Betsy** *nervously continues to cut the apples up into the bowl.*

He's an eye for you, of that there's no doubt. He admitted to sowing hemp seed by our door. You've gone red, girl.

**Betsy** (*quietly*)  I haven't, have I?

**Anne**  Scarlet. (*After a moment's pause. Turning, walking to the dresser.*) Is there not a boy at 'Thorpe who takes your fancy?

**Betsy**  I like it here.

**Anne** *takes a bowl off the dresser, she walks to an earthenware casket below the window ledge.*

**Anne**  Sometime soon we must sit down and talk about your future.

**Betsy**  Why?

**Anne**  One day you'll want a home of your own. (*Lifting the top off the casket.*) We must find someone suitable who'll give you that.

*The casket is full of flour.* **Anne** *proceeds to spoon some into the bowl.*

**Betsy**  I'd like to talk to aunt.

**Anne**  Would you?

**Betsy**  Yes. (*Hesitantly.*) I want to know the truth about me. I know I'm not your niece.

*A slight pause.*

Aunt, I've been reading your diaries.

**Anne**  Good.

**Anne** *replaces the top on the casket. She takes the bowl of flour to the table.*

(*Brightly*)   This war with France is making us all uppity. (*After a moment's pause.*) We'll talk soon, girl.

**Anne** *puts butter into the bowl and starts to mix it into the flour with her hands.* **Betsy** *finishes cutting the apples and starts to peel the carrot.*

**Betsy**  I wish they'd come. At least we'd know.

**Anne**  What a terrible thing to say.

*The song thrush sings.*

**Betsy** D'you think Squire Boulby knows what's happening?

**Anne** He is our Landlord. He sits in The House of Commons, with Mister Pitt.

**Betsy** I wonder why France wants to come here?

**Anne** To take our land from us.

**Betsy** I hate them.

**Betsy** *finishes peeling the carrot, she starts to chop it into the wooden bowl.*

**Anne** Have you ever thought why we bear hatred, Betsy?

**Betsy** What?

**Anne** And time exaggerates so, doesn't it?

**Betsy** *has finished cutting the carrot, she starts to peel and chop the onion.*

**Betsy** What d'you mean.

**Anne** I've been thinking about what you said las' night, about the fisherman with two heads. Our hatred for Bay Town is still growing. What happened, happened twenty years ago, not this day. You weren't even born.

**Betsy** I know.

**Anne** It's up to the young folk to put an end to it. And yet it's the young folk who are the worst.

*A few tears come into* **Betsy***'s eyes.*

What's the matter?

**Betsy** The onion. (*Screaming.*) A mouse!

**Betsy** *jumps onto the bench.*

**Anne** Where?

**Betsy** (*pointing*) Goyn beneath the dresser.

**Anne** (*looking at* **Betsy**) Don't be silly, girl, and come down.

**Betsy** *slowly gets off the bench.*

(*Still mixing the pastry*) Where's that silly cat?

**Betsy** *puts the chopped onion into the wooden bowl.*

**Betsy** Was there any other gossip at Fylingthorpe?

**Anne** I tried to stop some men gambling.

*A slight pause.*

Farmer Wood was there. Hirin' faggers t'mend his barn roof. I pity the faggers, he's a worse temper than John.

**Betsy** *puts the chopped pig meat into the bowl.*

Oh, and Wilf Meadow's wife has had her baby. During the storm of all nights.

**Betsy** What was it?

**Anne** A girl. They're going to risk the wrath of the village and call her Anne after me.

**Betsy** *smiles. She picks up a wooden spoon and starts to stir the mixture together in the bowl.*

I promised them a silver guinea. His son is coming to collect it this afternoon.

**Anne** *is making pastry.* **Betsy** *is stirring the mixture in the wooden bowl.*

*The lights slowly fade to blackout.*


Scene Four

*The beach and town at Robin Hood's Bay. The same morning.*

*A beach. Sand, stones, pebbles, driftwood, and seaweed. Towards the back the sand becomes soily and the ground grassy. Standing on the grass is the house belonging to* **Robert** *and* **Molly Storm**. *The house is made of stone with a brick slated roof. On the roof is a chimney-pot and small wisps of smoke can be seen drifting from it. The house has a door, painted green, with sash windows either side. On the sand, a short distance from the house, is a bench and two wicker baskets.*

*The sun is high in the sky. A strong bright light.*

**Molly Storm** *is sitting on the bench. She is shelling various sea creatures (crabs, limpets, whelks, mussels, oysters, etc.) with a sharp knife.*

**Molly** *is a plump, tallish woman of forty one. She has a rough, earthy*

*face, and straggling hair. Her hands and face are brown and dried
from the sun. Despite the heat she is over dressed and her clothes are of
a poor quality; several petticoats, a gown, an apron which is dirty, and
a bonnet; she is not wearing shoes.*

**Molly** *takes a limpet from one basket, removes the shell, the shell drops
onto the sand, and places the flesh in the second basket.*

**Mary** *enters walking across the grass towards the house. Her canvas
bag is on her shoulder. She knocks at the door.* **Molly** *looks up from
her work.*

**Molly**  Yeh, wha' is it?

**Mary**  This your 'ouse, Mistress?

**Molly**  Aye.

**Mary**  Want yer windas cleanin'?

**Molly**  I 'ave 'ands f'that mesell.

**Mary**  F'a penny?

**Molly**  Like yer thoughts, eh?

**Mary**  D'know.

**Molly**  A did 'em mesell not two days since.

**Mary**  (*disappointed*)  Oh.

**Molly**  You the boy livin' on the beach?

**Mary**  Yeh.

**Molly**  Yer bin goyn roun' all the houses?

**Mary**  Yeh.

**Molly**  Thess n'pennies fo'yer here. Thess 'ardly a coin f'us.

**Mary** *hesitates for a moment, she decides to stay.*

**Mary**  Where's all the men?

**Molly**  The're at the wreck. What's left of 'er.

**Mary**  Any work wi' them, Mistress.

**Molly**  Yer ears mus' need a clean, I've told yer.

**Mary**  Will the' be back soon?

**Molly**  The'll be back as fancy tekks 'em. Or the tide comes in.

The'll be drunk, I imagine. Very drunk. The first thing the' found this mornin' was the Port Wine.

**Mary** (*walking down towards* **Molly**) I could do wi' a drink.

**Molly** Drink ain' f'lads o'your years, it's a ruinous thing.

**Mary** *is standing near* **Molly**.

D'yer stay where yer not wanted?

**Mary** (*shrugging*) D'know.

**Molly** Go t'the farmers'n pester them.

**Mary** Gi'us a drink, Mistress.

**Molly** (*smiling*) Yer a bright'n a half, aren't yer? Bright as a silver button on a rich farmer's coat.

**Mary** *smiles*.

Jus' like one o'my lads, you are. I imagine 'is cheek'll do fer 'im an' all. The army took 'im. 'Eard a sound, nor seen a sight, f'six months. Poor little beggar.

**Mary** *sits down on the sand*.

It's one less mouth t'feed.

*A slight pause.*

Don' yer wish you were a farmer?

**Mary** *shrugs*.

Thess one farmer up there got so much money 'e built a barn o'gold t'keep it in. They reckon it's watched over by hobgoblins from India. (*After a moment's pause.*) Thess me left, 'ere.

**Molly** *smiles to herself*.

We're equal when we die, except f'the coffin.

**Mary** (*after a moment's pause*) What yer doin'?

**Molly** A'll mekk a big pie wi' these.

**Mary** Never eaten owt like 'em.

**Molly** (*smiling*) Bright, but not used t'the world, eh?

**Mary** Aint bin by the sea before.

**Molly** 'Aven't yer?

**Mary** *shakes her head.*

Well I never.

**Mary** It were like seein' a big monster when a first came.

**Molly** Were it?

**Mary** A didn' know what it was.

**Molly** Rum'n, rum'n.

**Mary** Yer wha'?

**Molly** Yer a rum'n, boy.

**Mary** No one'd telled me before.

*The bugle-like call of a herring-gull, as the bird flies over their heads.*

**Molly** Yer do what the sea sez. Yer don't argue wi' it. Too many lives're lost. The sea's calm t'day. So calm yer can 'ardly 'ear it.

*They listen. Silence.*

But there it is look, it's still there. It's foolin' yer.

**Mary** *looks at the sea. The bugle-like call of the herring-gull, as the bird flys back over their heads.*

The herring-gull knows when it's going t'be stormy, 'e goes inland. That's 'ow we knew about the storm las' night. We were waitin' for it. (*Looking at the sky.*) The're all back this mornin', shrewd as the writers of books.

**Molly** *puts down the knife, she reaches down to the bottom of her petticoats and lifts them up. Underneath, lying on the sand, is a small baby.* **Molly** *picks him up.*

Keep 'im from the sun.

**Molly** *opens her gown. The baby suckles at her breast.*

I should be passed 'avin' bairnes b'now.

**Mary** *watches.*

This one's good as gold. What d'you reckon to us 'ere?

**Mary** D'know.

**Molly** D'know much, d'yer?

**Mary** Suppose not.

**Molly** We don't see many strangers. Yer've got t'row t'Whitby f'that. D'yer know Whitby?

**Mary** *shakes her head.*

Whitby's a fine large town with a big harbour. (*Pointing.*) Up the coast, about four mile beyon' Bay Ness. We row there t'the markets. There yer might get yersell some work, on the big fishing boats. Can yer read'n write?

**Mary** *shakes her head.*

A wish a c'd say I could. Are yer God fearing?

**Mary** *nods.*

It's wise t', God is master o' the sea. Heard o'John Wesley?

**Mary** *shakes her head.*

Mister Wesley came 'ere. If yer see 'im, you scatter. Like strong drink 'e brought religious ruin t'the town. Except the men don't reckon so. Mekken 'em feel bad wi' 'is preachin'. Tellin' 'em t'mekk peace wi' the farmers. It's the farmers who wronged us. Fillin' their 'eads wi' guilt. A'd curse the name o' John Wesley but The Lord might strike me. Fearin' God is one thing, John Wesley summat else. Not that boys like you know owt.

**Mary** Is there a fisherman wi' two heads, Mistress?

**Molly** Thess a farmer wi' five hands – mekkin' light work of everything. 'N' another wi' a tongue that spits fire. Mind, the' all d'that. Why?

**Mary** Jus' wondered.

**Mary** *takes a cloth rag from her pocket. The rag is filthy.* **Mary** *mops her brow.*

**Molly** Yer hot?

**Mary** Aye.

**Molly** It is hot t'day. The earth's an oven. A d'know which is muckier, you or the rag.

**Mary** *puts the rag away.*

I'm a winter woman if the truth be told. 'N' when it gets

t'winter, a long f'the summer.

**Molly** *looks along the coast towards Bay Ness.*

What're your eyes like, boy?

**Mary** (*following* **Molly***'s gaze*)  The sea's shiny.

**Molly**  I'm as blind as a bat. Is that our cobbles comin' back?

**Mary**  What's a cobble?

**Molly**  Fishin' cobble, our rowin' boats.

**Mary** (*looking at* **Molly**)  The've bin at the wrecked boat, 'ave the?

**Molly**  They should 'ave some plunder wi' 'em.

**Mary**  What's plunder?

**Molly**  Stuff the'll've tekkn off. Plates, cups, bowls. Mekk our life easier.

**Mary** (*looking along the coast*)  Thess a load of 'em.

**Molly**  A'the rowin' straight?

**Mary**  The're in a line.

**Molly**  I wondered 'ow drunk the' were. I 'ope not very drunk. (*Mopping her brow with her hand.*) Yer mekkin' me swet now, rum'n. (*Looking down the beach towards Bay Ness, squinting.*) Who's this hurryin' down the sand?

**Mary** *looks.*

The're back. I'd get off if I were you.

**Mary** *stays put.*

(*Taking the baby off her nipple*) Sorry, sweet'n.

**Molly** *stands up, the baby in her arms.*

(*Calling*) What yer got?

*A slight pause.*

What yer got? Owt good?

**Robert** *and* **Joe** *enter from Bay Ness. They are dressed for the sun in breeches, shirts and neck-ties. There is nothing on their feet.*

**Robert** *and* **Joe** *are carrying between them a long wooden crate.*

What's in there?

**Robert** (*his voice booming*)  Yer'll get a shock, Molly. We hurried back.

**Robert** *and* **Joe** *put the crate down.*

**Molly**  What's in it?

**Robert**  The rest're in the cobbles.

**Molly**  What?

**Robert** (*taking the top off the crate*)  We found crates'n crates of these, Molly.

*The crate is full of infantry muskets.*

**Robert** *picks one up.*

The French're here.

**Molly** (*taking a step back*)  Oh, The Lord God, whatever next.

**Robert**  An' do yerself up, woman.

**Molly** *pulls her gown over her naked breast.* **Mary** *stands up.*

**Joe** (*calmly*)  We don't know it's the French, Robert.

**Robert** (*his voice booming*)  I do. They're hidin' in the caves'n woods. I saw somethin' earlier. (*Trying to cock the musket.*) I'm ready for 'em.

**Molly** (*to* **Joe**)  What else is there?

**Joe**  There's no sign of a living or dead soul. They either jumped'n were drowned –

**Robert**  The didn' jump.

**Joe**  Or somehow they've got ashore.

**Robert**  The' here, waitin' for us. (*Not succeeding with the musket.*) The' don't frighten me.

**Molly**  What're we goyn t'do?

**Robert**  Fight 'em off.

**Joe** (*calmly*)  We do what we came ahead for.

**Robert** (*walking towards the town*)  I'll go and tell 'em to ring the church bell.

**Joe** (*calling after him*)  And come straight back. Tell everyone yer see, this is where we'll meet.

**Robert**  Aye. (*Holding up the musket.*) I'm tekkin' this with me. Keep the French from my wife, Joe.

**Robert** *exits.*

**Molly**  Is the boat badly wrecked?

**Joe**  The rocks're right through her hull. (*Putting the top on the crate.*) Can yer help me wi' this. I want it hidden and safe.

**Molly**  D'you think they're watching us, Joe?

**Joe**  If they are they'll show themselves soon.

**Mary**  Who's watchin' us?

**Joe**  You come too, boy.

**Molly** *and* **Joe** *pick up the crate.* **Molly** *has the baby in her other*


*They exit with the crate towards the town.*
**Mary** *stays and watches them go.*
*The bugle-like call of a herring-gull as the bird flies overhead.*

**Mary** *stoops down and picks up her canvas bag.*

**Mary** (*calling*)  All right.

**Mary** *stoops down and picks up her canvas bag.*

(*Calling*)  All right.

**Mary** *walks towards the town, as she does so a gorilla enters, walking on all fours from the direction of Bay Ness.*

*In a few moments* **Mary** *will christen the gorilla* **Stockton**. *He is black and furry: a real gorilla. He is wearing a blue woollen sailor's jumper.*

**Stockton** *sneezes, a kind of snort.* **Mary** *hears this, stops, and turns. She steps back a pace in fear.* **Stockton** *looks briefly at* **Mary** *and sits down on the sand.*

Who're you?

*A slight pause.*

Where did you come from?

*A slight pause.*

(*Pointing*) I was supposed t'be goyn wi' them.

**Stockton** *is watching* **Mary** *from the corner of his eye.*

I'm not frightened, 'r you? (*Taking a few steps towards* **Stockton**.) A don' want t'harm yer. I'm friendly.

**Stockton** *sneezes.* **Mary** *stops.*

*A slight pause.*

**Stockton** *looks at* **Mary** *from the corner of his eye.*

Yer shy, aren't yer?

**Stockton** *stands and walks on all fours towards* **Mary**. **Mary** *backs off.*

(*Frightened.*) No, don't come near me.

**Stockton** *stops and sits down again.*

A thought yer were goyn t'get me.

**Stockton** *watches* **Mary** *from the corner of his eye.*

Yer weren't, were yer? (*Warily taking a few steps towards him.*) You're my friend. (*Another step.*) We'll both be friends.

**Stockton** *sneezes.*

'Ave you got a cold?

**Mary** *reaches out and touches* **Stockton's** *head. She moves warily forward, stroking him.* **Stockton** *enjoys it.*

I'm goyn to call you Stockton. After where a come from. I'm goyn t'look after you.

**Mary** *kneels down and continues to stroke him.* **Stockton** *watches her from the corner of his eye.*

You'n me, we're together.

**Stockton** *sneezes.*

(*Pulling a face.*) Er, yer sprayed me wi' water, yer have got a cold.

**Stockton** *stands up, walks away a few paces, and sits down again.*

Where yer goyn? Don' yer like me?

**Stockton** *lets out a loud call.* **Mary** *steps back.*

Don' do that. I don' like it when yer do that.

*A slight pause.*

(*Walking towards* **Stockton**, *warily*) Is that all yer can say? Can yer say owt else?

**Stockton** *is watching* **Mary** *from the corner of his eye.* **Mary** *reaches* **Stockton** *and strokes him again.*

**Molly** *enters from the town, she has the baby in one hand, a piece of wood in the other. She stops.*
**Mary** *puts her arms round* **Stockton**'s *neck and tries to pull him.*

Come on, come wi' me, we'll go t'my tent.

**Stockton** *doesn't move.*

(*Pulling him again*) Why won't yer come? Yer heavy.

**Mary** *looks up and sees* **Molly.**

**Molly** Stay with 'im boy.

**Mary** (*standing up*) 'E won't 'arm yer. 'E's my friend, 'e's friendly.

**Stockton** *walks on all fours towards* **Molly**. **Molly** *raises the piece of wood and backs off.*

**Molly** (*screaming*) Ge' back, ge' back, ge' back.

*Before* **Stockton** *reaches* **Molly** *he sits down again.*

(*Screaming*) Don't do that again.

**Mary** (*going to* **Stockton**) Why don't yer like 'im?

**Robert** *and* **Joe** *enter from Bay Ness. They have a large fishing net stretched out between them.* **Robert** *also has the musket.*

**Robert** Joe?

**Joe** I don't know, Robert.

**Mary** (*looking at* **Robert** *and* **Joe**) What's goyn on. (*Stroking* **Stockton** *confused*) I've seen one before. In a fair.

**Robert** *spits.*

**Robert** Frenchman!

**Mary** (*looking between the three of them*) No, it did tricks. Like standin' on it's 'ead. Then it collected pennies from people.

**Joe** (*calmly*) It looks like an animal.

**Mary** It is. Honest.

**Molly** (*aggressively*) The boy's lying.

**Mary** (*looking between the three of them*) 'N' I'm not a boy, I'm a girl really.

**Robert** Now the boy sez 'e's a girl.

**Mary** I am a girl. I've jus' been pretending. These were all the clothes I 'ad.

**Joe** What's your name?

**Mary** Mary. Honest.

**Robert** Boys aren't called Mary.

**Mary** I am.

**Robert** (*his voice booming*) The boy's a spy f'the Frenchman. He's bin waitin' fo'im. Why yer livin' on the beach?

**Stockton** *gets up, he walks on all fours in a small circle.*
**Molly, Robert** and **Joe** *step back.* **Stockton** *sits down again. He watches them all from the corner of his eye.*

**Mary** (*looking between the three of them*) A ran away see. With me brother. Only me brother died o'the fever, so a took 'is clothes.

**Molly** The boy's a liar.

**Mary** No. A left me brother in a hedge back somewhere.

**Robert** *spits.*

**Robert** Frenchman!

**Stockton** *stands up and walks a pace towards* **Robert**. *He sits down again.*

(*Agressively, frightened*) Stop 'im doin' that.

**Mary** A can't. (*Going to* **Stockton**.) Yer musn't do that, the' don't like it.

*The church bell starts to toll from the distance.*

**Robert** What're we goyn t'do, Joe?

**Molly** The boy's a spy.

**Joe**  If he was armed he'd have tried to shoot us by now. (*To* **Mary**.) Where did 'e come from?

**Mary** (*pointing*)  Down there. His name's Stockton.

**Joe**  Where're the rest of them?

**Mary**  A don't know.

**Molly**  The boy's lying.

**Stockton** *lets out a loud call.*

**Robert** (*stepping back*)  He's goyn to attack us, Joe, 'e's callin' 'is friends.

**Joe**  Tell us the truth, child, where are they?

**Mary** *is beginning to feel upset, she shakes her head.*

**Robert** (*to* **Joe**)  Shall I shoot 'im?

**Stockton** *lets out a loud call.*

They're all around us, Joe.

**Joe**  Is he a Frenchman?

**Mary** *looks at* **Joe**, *she has tears in her eyes.*

(*Insistent*)  Is he?

**Mary** *nods.*

Why did you bring 'im 'ere?

**Stockton** *lets out a loud call. He stands up and walks quickly on all fours in the direction of the town.*

**Molly** (*screaming*)  He's escapin'.

**Robert** *and* **Joe** *chase after* **Stockton**. *They throw the fishing net over him.* **Stockton** *yelps, falls, and starts to rush blindly in all directions. In doing so he tangles himself further in the net.*
**Molly**, **Robert** *and* **Joe** *back off watching.* **Stockton** *comes to a final halt, he can move no more.*
**Robert** *points the gun at* **Stockton**.

**Robert**  We've got 'im, we've captured a Frenchman.

*The church clock is still tolling.*
**Mary** *has tears in her eyes.* **Stockton** *is panting. They are all still. The lights fade to blackout.*

# Act Two

Scene One

*Middlewood. Twenty years earlier. Mid afternoon of Christmas Eve, 1777.*

*A sheep enclosure (clearing) in the middle of the wood. A rough stone wall runs in a U-shaped arc round the perimeter of the stage. In the wall, to the left, is a gateway with a wooden gate. Behind the wall, Oak, Ash, and Sycamore trees are growing. The enclosure is free of any woody vegetation. To the right is a small low stone building (a small barn) with an open front and a sloping thatch roof. The barn is stacked with hay.*

*There is thick snow on the ground, and on the trees. The snow has drifted heavily against the stone wall and a path has had to be cleared to the gate.*

*The sky is thick with snow. It is quite dark.*

**Joe** *is standing at the opening to the barn. He has a book, wrapped in an old cloth, in his hand.*

**Joe** *doesn't quite look the twenty years younger; his face is pinched and old-mannish, but it is somehow cleaner, brighter. His skin is white. His clothes are of very poor quality and he is inadequately dressed for the cold; breeches, shirt, waistcoat, neck-tie, jacket. He has no shoes on his feet and instead has bound old pieces of cloth round them with string.*

**Joe** *blows into his hands, and stamps his feet, to keep warm. He hears someone coming and steps back into the barn.*

**Richard Wheatley** *enters followed by the young* **John**. **Richard** *is carrying a dead sheep across his shoulders.* **John** *is carrying a spade.*

**Richard** *is a tall, strong, burly man of forty-four. He has broad shoulders, a fat gut, and a powerful, intelligent face. He is dressed richly for the cold in boots, stockings, breeches, shirt, waistcoat, jacket, top coat, and a hat.*

*The young* **John** *is twelve. As yet he shows little sign of the donkey-like adult he will become. He has a clean face with alert eyes. His clothes are of good quality; boots, trousers, shirt, waistcoat, jacket, and a top coat.*

**Richard** *and* **John** *stop.*

**Richard** Who's there hiding?

**Joe** (*coming out from the barn*) Me, Mister Wheatley.

**Richard** It's you, Joe. Good afternoon.

**Joe** (*nodding, shyly*) Afternoon t'yer both.

**Richard** Might I ask what your purpose is?

**Joe** (*politely*) I'm waitin' f'Emma.

**Richard** Is that all?

**Joe** We meet 'ere, Mister Wheatley.

**Richard** (*smiling*) Up to the devil's mischief, John.

**John** *smiles.*

I hope it's not mischief yer up to.

**Joe** We've bin courtin' f'over a year.

**Richard** Remember whose land you're on.

**Joe** (*nodding slightly*) A will.

**Richard** Don't trespass more than yer need.

**Joe** No, Mister Wheatley.

**Richard** There are sheep stealers in this part of Yorkshire. Moving north from Scarborough. The snow will be stopping them – but, I like to know who's on my land.

**Joe** *nods.*
**Richard** *drops the sheep to the ground.*

(*Brightly*) So yer meet the lass here in the cold?

**Joe** Aye.

**Joe** *blows into his hands.*

**Richard** Is there nowhere else where it's warmer?

**Joe** It were warm in summer, Mister Wheatley.

**Richard** I did my courtin' in all weathers.

**Joe** *quietly stamps his feet.*

'N' 'ave yer nothin' f'yer feet?

**Joe** *is silent.*

Why don't yer meet 'er at the farm? It would be better than here.

**Joe** *stops. He is still.*

The Mistress wouldn't mind yer usin' her kitchen. I'm sure of that.

**Joe**   It's kind of yer, Mister Wheatley.

**Richard**   What's the matter? Our kitchen's not good enough, John?

**Joe**   I don' mind the cold.

**Richard**   The look of you tells another story. Emma's a fine lass. What about her and the weather?

**Joe**   (*quietly stamping his feet again*)   She don' mind, Mister Wheatley.

**Richard**   Have you asked her, Joe?

**Joe**   Of course.

**Joe** *looks down at the snow.*

**Richard**   Emma's a good maid, the best maid we've had. I don't want to see 'er wronged.

**Joe**   (*looking up*)   I love 'er, Mister Wheatley.

**Richard**   As long as yer do.

**Emma Braye** *enters between the trees.*

**Emma** *is a slim, attractive woman of twenty-six, and although her face has a mature, hard-worked look to it, there has remained something vibrant and girlish.*

*She is dressed for the cold in* **Anne**'s *cast off clothing; shows, a gown, a grey cape, and a bonnet.*

**Emma** *hides behind a tree. They do not see her.*

Come to the kitchen next time.

**Joe**   I'll tell 'er. I will.

**Richard**   I hear you're a good worker, Joe? (*Walking towards him.*) 'N' you say you love Emma.

**Richard** *stands beside* **Joe**.

Is being wed to the girl in your mind?

**Joe**  One day, Mister Wheatley.

**Richard**  Is it indeed.

**Joe**  I'd come t'yer first, f'yer permission. Emma's parents bein' dead, 'n' you lookin' after 'er. 'Avin' no folks of 'er own.

**Richard**  There'd be trouble from Mistress if Emma was to leave us.

**Joe** *looks down at the snow.*

If Emma was t'stay, 'n' help in the kitchen now'n again, 'n' help in the dairy with the butter makin'. But set up home with you in one of my cottages – would you com'n work for me?

**Joe** *looks up. He is silent.*

(*Turning to* **John**) There's an offer, John, isn' it?

**John** *smiles.*

A farmer's life is different from yours. What d'yer say, Joe?

**Joe** (*politely, nervously*) I d'know, Mister Wheatley.

**Richard**  I'm offering yer the chance t'better yerself.

**Joe** (*quietly stamping his feet*) A can't think in the cold.

**Richard** (*turning, walking back to* **John**) Think about it. Let me know. But don't think too long.

**Joe**  A will.

**Richard** *puts his arm round* **John**. **Emma** *is listening intently behind the tree.*

**Richard**  We're looking for a shepherd.

**Joe**  What 'appened t'Tom Meadows?

**Richard**  'E died las' week.

**Joe**  Poor ol' Tom Meadows.

**Richard**  If I don't tekk you I'll tekk his son Wilf.

**John** (*looking at his father*) Yer haven't told him the pay.

**Richard**  You tell him.

**John**  Nine pounds a year.

**Joe**  Did 'e die from cold?

**Richard**  This winter is taking many.

**Joe**  The old an' the sick, Mister Wheatley.

**Richard**  Aye.

**Joe**  If I'll be your shepherd, what 'appens t'young Wilf?

**Richard**  He'll join the faggers at 'Thorpe.

**Joe**  An' 'is family will lose their cottage?

**Richard**  The parish cares f'the poor, Joe. I'm not a ruthless man. (*Moving from* **John**, *standing back.*) I've lost six of my sheep in this snow. This one found shelter against a wall, the snow blew in an' covered 'er.

**Joe**  She'll feed you, Mister Wheatley.

**Richard**  Aye, but she'll bear no lamb.

**Joe**  (*gaining courage*)  We're starving at Bay Town. The sea's froze over, our boats're stuck in the ice.

**Emma**  *puts her hands in front of her eyes to hide them.*

**Richard**  I've seen them.

**Emma**  *takes her hands away.*

**Joe**  We can't fish. Only by mekkin' holes. An' dangling a hand line.

**Richard**  'Ave yer nothin' put by?

*A slight pause.*

Come t'me, Joe, I'll feed yer.

**Joe**  The whole town needs feedin'.

*A slight pause.*

**Richard**  I didn't know you were so bad.

**Joe**  Since the snow came.

**Richard**  A month?

**Joe**  Summat like, Mister Wheatley.

**John**  I saw the girls skating.

**Richard** 'N' yer starving?

**Joe**  Near starving.

**Richard** (*after a moment's pause*)  Thess nothing I can do, Joe. Yer must plan.

**Joe** *looks at the snow for a moment.*

**Joe** (*looking back up*)  A feel like begging Mister Wheatley.

**Richard**  Take my job.

**Joe** (*strong in his mind*)  A'll think on.

**Richard**  You do that.

*A slight pause.*

(*Picking up the dead sheep. Brightly*)  Come on, John, let's be home t'your mother. She'll be thinkin' we've died in a drift ourselves.

**Richard** *carries the sheep towards the gate.* **John** *follows with the spade.*

Open the gate, Joe.

**Joe** *goes to the gate and opens it.*
**Richard** *and* **John** *exit towards the farm.*
**Emma** *comes out from behind the tree.*

**Emma**  Joe.

**Joe** *looks up, sees her.*

I 'eard. I was 'idin'.

**Joe** (*turning, walking away from the gate and* **Emma**)  Is hatred too strong a word f'what I feel about 'im?

**Emma** *comes through the gate, she stops.*

**Emma**  Yer cold, Joe.

**Joe** (*after a moment's pause. Turning to her. Half smiling*)  Warmer with you.

*They walk towards each other. They kiss. They embrace.* **Emma** *rubs her hands vigorously up and down his back.*

**Emma**  I'll 'ave yer warm as an oven in a minute.

**Joe**  Oh, that's nice.

*They continue the embrace for a moment and then break it.*

'E dun' alf mekk me mad.

**Emma** *holds out her hand,* **Joe** *takes it.*

A seem t'wither away when a see 'im.

**Emma**  Yer don't. I expected 'is temper any time.

**Joe**  What d'yer mean?

**Emma**  Yer stand up to 'im. 'E's a foul temper. 'E' likes yer.

**Joe**  Oh.

**Emma** (*smiling*) Don't be surprised.

**Joe**  Can' 'elp it.

**Emma**  Why yer surprised?

**Joe**  A thought a weren't me in front of 'im.

**Emma**  'E ain' a bad sort, Joe.

**Joe**  Don' start.

**Emma**  Wait on.

**Emma** *smiles.*

**Joe**  What yer want t'say? Emma –

**Emma**  I 'eard 'im about the job.

**Joe** (*turning, walking away a pace or two*) Thought that was it.

**Emma** (*walking to* **Joe**) F' year or two.

**Joe** (*firmly*) No.

**Emma** (*looking at him*) Please, Joe.

**Joe** *turns and walks away a few paces.*

**Joe** (*turning to her*) I ain't changin' the plans. We're leavin' 'ere. I'm tekkin' yer.

**Emma**  I'm not sayin' change 'em.

**Joe**  What are yer then?

**Emma**  Put 'em off f'a bit.

**Joe**  That's change 'em t'me.

**Emma** *looks at* **Joe**.

We're goyn in the spring.

**Emma**  Yer know in the autumn, Joe – what we've bin doin'?

**Joe** *looks blank*.

Yer do. Not now cos it's t'cold.

**Joe**  What?

**Emma**  (*touching her stomach*)  I've a child in 'ere.

**Joe**  A don't believe yer.

**Emma**  (*calmly*)  Yer'll 'ave to, cos it's so.

**Joe**  Who said?

**Emma**  Mistress Wheatley tol' me.

**Joe**  She's tellin' yer lies, Emma.

**Emma**  She aint, Joe.

**Joe**  Wait 'till a see Robert Storm, a were swallowin' the ten worms.

**Emma**  A tol' Mistress Wheatley, she said that don't do nowt. It's in me belly, Joe. It mekks a difference to us now.

**Joe**  Why?

**Emma**  F'me. 'Avin' the child in my own village.

**Joe**  Course it don't, Emma.

**Emma**  It do t'me.

**Joe**  Yer enjoyed it right enough.

**Emma**  (*after a moment's pause*)  That's not like you, Joe.

*Silence between them for a few moments.* **Emma** *walks to* **Joe.**

**Joe**  (*stepping back a pace*)  No, a don't want yer.

*They stop a short distance apart. Silence for a moment.*

Course a want yer, a don't want the bairne.

**Emma**  Mebbe it'll die.

**Joe**  (*after a moment's pause*)  Did yer tell Mistress Wheatley who the father were?

**Emma** I 'ad to.

**Joe** Is that why 'e offered me the job?

**Emma** 'E don't know. (*After a moment's pause.*) She said it could be worse. You bein' the fine man you are. If not s'fine f'doin' that.

**Joe** (*after a moment's pause*) We'll 'ave t'wait then. (*Heartfelt.*) I wanted t'go t'the city, Emma. I hate this place.

**Emma** Don't, Joe.

**Joe** It's easy f'you. You've food in your belly. A child as well I suppose.

**Emma** It aint easy.

**Joe** Waitin' fo'yer, a were all merry. Now it don't seem like Christmas Eve.

**Emma** Will yer tekk 'is job?

**Joe** A can't, Emma.

**Emma** F'me, at Christmas?

**Joe** I'm a fisherman.

**Emma** 'E'd treat yer well.

**Joe** (*turning, walking away a pace*) Course 'e wouldn't.

**Emma** 'E would, Joe.

**Joe** (*turning to* **Emma**) The way he's treated Bay. The way we've been treated.

**Emma** A were talkin' about you.

**Joe** All this land were common land! Look at it now! Fences on it! It belongs to the farmers! That's why we're starving!

*Silence.*

(*Still shaking with anger*) I aint gonna say sorry either. Not while 'is stomach is full.

*A slight pause.*

If yer want me, yer come t'Bay. Cos I aint comin' t'Thorpe.

*Silence.*

**Emma** *looks down and walks a pace or two away from* **Joe**.
*Silence.*
**Joe** *blows into his hands.*

**Emma** (*looking up*) I'll go then, Joe. Are we still meetin' on Boxin' Day?

**Joe** If yer want.

**Emma** I can get angry too yer know.

**Joe** (*staring at her*) Why don' yer?

**Emma** (*after a moment's pause*) Per'aps a can't get angry then.

**Joe** This land belonged to all of us, Emma. Fisherman 'n' farmers alike. The farmers took it.

**Emma** It were by Act of Parliament in London.

**Joe** What d'we know about London? Them folk in London don't give us food.

**Joe** *blows into his hands.*

**Emma** Squire Boulby took the land not Mister Wheatley.

**Joe** 'E tills the soil, don' 'e? Puts 'is livestock on it.

**Emma** 'N' 'e pays the rent.

**Joe** You 'ave t'be starvin' to understand.

*A slight pause.*

I ain' eaten t'day, Emma. A didn' eat yesterday.

**Emma** *looks down at the snow.*

If I 'ad, a don't suppose a'd care.

**Emma** (*looking up, gently*) A reckon yer would, Joe.

**Joe** A want food.

**Emma** Why won't yer tekk 'is job then?

**Joe** Inside me, a can't.

**Emma** Why?

**Joe** *is silent.*

Yer too proud.

**Joe** (*after a moment's pause*) I want to.

**Emma** Do it, Joe.

**Joe** No.

*Silence.*

**Emma** Talking never helps us, does it?

**Emma** *walks to* **Joe**. **Joe** *takes her hand. They kiss. They embrace.*

**Joe** A brought the book wi me.

**Emma** A noticed.

**Joe** Thess some words a don' understand.

**Emma** Let's look at 'em then.

*They break the embrace.* **Joe** *walks to a log which is lying on the ground, he clears the snow off the top of it with his hand. He sits down.* **Emma** *sits down beside him.* **Joe** *starts to unwrap the book from the cloth.*

*It is Jethro Tull's 'The Horse-Hoeing Husbandry'. The book is marked with little slips of paper, he opens it at page 73.*

**Joe** Thess a word 'ere. (*He puts his finger on the line and reads out the sentence.*) All weeds, as such, are perni-ice-ous; but some much more than others. Perni-ice-ous?

**Emma** *looks at the word.*

**Emma** A don't know. It mebbe means like bad.

**Joe** Bad?

**Emma** Well yer don' want weeds in a field, d'yer?

**Joe** That don't make sense.

**Emma** A'm only trying, Joe.

**Joe** (*reading the sentence again*) All weeds, as such, are bad; but some much more than others. Mebbe it does.

**Emma** I'll 'ave to ask Mrs Wheatley.

**Joe** A thought yer knew every word.

**Emma** Don't be silly, Joe.

**Joe**  A thought yer did.

**Emma**  Thess more words than anyone can remember.

**Joe**  Don' tell me lies then.

**Emma**  What's the next one?

**Joe**  *turns to page 79. He puts his finger on the line and reads.*

**Joe**  Tis but of late years that turnips have been introduc'd as an improvement in the field. All sorts of land, when made fine by tillage, or by manure and tillage, will serve to produce turnips, but not equally; (*Enjoying himself.*) for chalky land is generally too dry (a turnip bein' a thirsty plant); and if they are too long in such dry poor soil before they get into rough leaf, the fly is very apt to destroy them, yet I have known them succeed on rough land, tho' rarely.

**Joe**  *takes his finger off the page and smiles.*

A've bin practisin' that bit.

**Emma**  *kisses* **Joe** *on the cheek.*

A'll soon know more words than you.

**Emma**  (*smiling, happy*) We're different, Joe.

**Joe**  Won' a?

**Emma**  Aye.

**Joe**  Then I'll teach 'em t'you. It'll be t'other way round.

**Emma**  Of course yer will.

**Joe**  What were yer sayin'?

**Emma**  A were sayin' we were different.

**Joe**  A will know more words, Emma, yer'll 'ave to accept that.

**Emma**  Can we 'ave one conversation, not two.

**Joe**  (*excited*) A did it, a did it. Me readin'.

**Emma**  *smiles.*

(*Looking at the front cover*) Jethro Tull's Horse-Hoeing Husbandry. Can't yer get me books about summat else? I'm sick o'farming.

**Emma**  They're the only books Mister Wheatley has.

**Joe**  Soon I'll know more about farmin' than 'e does.

**Emma** *smiles.*

(*Picking up a handful of powdery snow and throwing it into the air*) A did it, Emma. A didn' reckon a would.

**Emma**  I knew yer would.

**Joe**  Did yer? I didn't.

**Emma** (*smiling*)  I know, calm down.

**Joe**  A did it, a did it, a did it.

**Emma** *laughs.*

A did it, Emma.

**Joe** *laughs. They are both laughing.*

(*Standing up*) It's jus' 'avin' the confidence, isn' it? T'know the words. I ain't no fear now. I 'ave 'ad before.

**Emma** (*standing up*)  We belong in another world, Joe.

**Joe**  Yer what?

**Emma**  We ain't part o' this one.

**Joe** (*putting his hand on* **Emma**'s *stomach*)  Come wi' me t'the city.

**Emma**  I 'ave fears, Joe.

**Joe**  Yer wha'?

**Emma**  I 'ave fears.

**Joe**  Yer've learnt me, Emma.

**Emma**  Mistress Wheatley taught me.

**Joe**  I alwez reckoned it were me that were scared.

**Emma** (*shaking her head*)  No.

**Joe**  Mistress Wheatley is a good sort, ain't she?

**Emma**  The've given me a home.

*A slight pause.*

We're special, Joe. You'n me. We're special here. We can make another world, but at the farm.

**Joe** *looks down at the snow.*

We don't know what's at the city, do we?

**Joe** (*looking up*) No. (*After a moment's pause.*) Yer right. (*Turning, walking away a pace.*) I'm sick o'yer bein' right.

**Joe** *stops, turns, and walks back.*

All right, I'll tekk the job.

**Emma** (*smiling*) Joe.

**Joe** (*smiling*) Of course a will.

**Emma** (*hugging him*) Oh, Joe.

**Joe** Careful, yer'll knock me over.

**Emma** It is Christmas now.

**Joe** It were Christmas before.

**Emma** (*pulling back slightly from the embrace. Looking at him*) Think better of yerself. Alwez think better.

**Joe** (*smiling*) Yer goyn again, tellin' me what t'think. (*They hug.*) I suppose I'll learn t'like Mister Wheatley.

*They are still, holding one another.*
*The lights fade to blackout.*


Scene Two

*Middlewood. Mid afternoon of Boxing Day.*

*The sky is still thick with snow. It is quite dark.*

**Emma** *is near the barn waiting for* **Joe**. *She is stooping, making a snowball. Beside her is a box tied with a ribbon. She is wearing a red cloak, apart from this her clothes are the same.* **Emma** *puts the box under her arm and stands up with the snowball. She blows into her empty hand. She sees* **Joe** *coming and puts the snowball behind her back.*

**Joe** *enters hurrying nervously. He is out of breath. He looks once behind his back.*

**Joe** Did anyone follow yer?

**Emma** Eh?

**Joe** Did anyone follow yer?

**Emma** *smiles and throws the snowball. It hits him.*

(*Brushing the snow away*) Don' Emma.

**Emma** I'm sorry. A made it f'you.

**Joe** *grabs* **Emma**'s *hand.*

What's goyn on?

**Joe** *pulls* **Emma** *into the entrance way of the barn.*

What's 'appened?

**Joe** (*quietly*) Don' mekk a noise. (*Pleading.*) Please, Emma.

**Emma** (*quietly*)  Wha' is it?

**Joe** (*still catching his breath*) I'll tell yer in a minute. Where's Mister Wheatley?

**Emma** A d'know, 'e's round wi' the sheep somewhere. They all are. Why?

**Joe** Thess trouble. (*After taking a deep breath.*) Thess gonna be trouble.

**Emma** Get yer breath back'n tell us prop'ly.

**Joe** *takes a few deep breaths. He breathes more easily.*

**Joe** We've 'ad a meetin' in the Anchor. All of us.

**Emma** Yeh?

**Joe** D'know 'ow t'tell yer.

**Emma** Jus' tell us.

**Joe** We're goyn t'come'n raid the farms.

**Emma** Yer what?

**Joe** We're goyn t'com'n raid the farms.

**Emma** What fo'?

**Joe** Tekk back the land that were ours. Knock the fences over.

**Emma** Then what?

**Joe** It'll be our land like before.

**Emma**  Who said?

**Joe** *shrugs.*

**Joe**  We did. All of us.

**Emma**  You?

**Joe** *shrugs.*

**Joe**  Suppose me.

**Emma**  You said that?

**Joe**  We were all sat round, what could a'say?

**Emma** (*shaking her head*)  A don't believe yer.

**Joe**  Yer'd better.

**Emma**  'N' you said nowt?

**Joe** *looks at the snow for a moment.*

**Joe** (*looking back up*)  A wanted t'say we should come'n beg. A near got on me knees. A would a'done, a were a coward.

*A short silence.*

Yer don't understand, d'yer?

**Emma**  No. (*Walking out of the barn.*)  I thought yer were stronger than that.

**Joe**  Please come 'ere, Emma. If the' see yer. A were told not t'come.

**Emma** *walks back into the barn.*

Someone might've followed me.

*A slight pause.*

**Emma**  When d'they plan it?

**Joe**  T'night.

*A slight pause.*

**Emma**  One of us 'as got t'do summat.

*A slight pause.*

Are yer goyn t'tell Mister Wheatley?

**Joe** *looks down at the snow.*

Then yer not tekkin' is job.

*A slight pause.*

**Joe** You could come wi' me.

**Emma** *looks at* **Joe.**

*A short silence.*

**Emma** *takes the box from beneath her arm.*

**Emma** It's Boxing Day. I brought these from Mister Wheatley.

**Joe** *takes the box from her. He unties the ribbon and takes the lid off the box. He takes out a pair of* **Richard**'s *cast-off shoes.*

**Joe** A don' wan' 'em, Emma.

*He puts the shoes back in the box, and gives the box to* **Emma. Emma** *takes a small, neatly wrapped packet from her cloak pocket.*

**Emma** An' this is from me. It's not much.

**Joe** No thank you.

**Emma** *(tears swelling from her eyes)* Don' be so pig headed an' tekk it.

**Joe** *(taking the packet)* Thanks. I can smell it from here. *(He smells the packet.)* It's tobacco. *(After a moment's pause.)* I made you a brooch. From a piece of jet a found. I forgot it. *(He sniffs the tobacco.)* I'll enjoy smokin' this.

*He puts the packet in his waist-coat pocket.*

Yer wearin' a new cloak, aren't yer?

**Emma** *(showing it off, she is proud of the cloak.)* The Mistress gave it to me. It's her old one.

**Joe** It looks nice on yer.

*A short silence.*

**Emma** *(her tears gone, she has held them back)* We've a Frenchman comin' t'stay. It's good news, unlike yours.

**Joe** Oh aye?

**Emma** He's here to study our farms. A letter's come from Squire Boulby in London.

**Joe**  Yer'll hear talk of another country.

**Emma**  I'll be sent out, I expect. I'll go then, Joe.

**Emma** *walks from the barn towards the gate. After a moment* **Joe** *steps from the barn. He stops.*

**Joe**  Don't go, Emma.

**Emma** *turns to face him.*

Won't yer tell me you understand?

**Emma**  I can't, Joe, 'cos I don't.

**Joe** *gets down onto his knees.*

**Joe**  If I do this t'yer.

**Emma**  What for?

**Joe**  It's other people messed it up, not us.

**Emma**  It's us.

**Joe**  I'm on me knees, Emma. What more can a do?

**John** *enters running. He has a snowball in his hand which he throws at* **Emma**.
**Joe** *stands up.*
*The snowball hits* **Emma**.

**John** (*calling joyfully back the way he entered*)  I got her.

**Richard** *enters followed by* **Anne**.

Did you see it? I hit her.

**Anne** *looks twenty years younger; her whole appearance is of a more agile, sprightly woman. She is thinner, her hair has yet to grey. She is dressed for the cold in shoes, a gown, a new red cloak, gloves and a bonnet.*

*The sun starts to come out from behind the clouds.*

**Anne**  I hope Emma didn't mind.

**John**  You didn't mind, did you, Emma?

**Emma**  No.

**John** (*bending down, ready to make a snowball*)  Let's have a snowball fight.

**Anne**  Not now, John.

**John** (*disappointed*)  Oh, why?

**Anne**  Because I'm your mother, 'n' I said so.

**John** *looks at his father.*

**Richard**  Do as your mother sez.

**John** *pulls a disappointed face and stands up.*
*The sun is shining through the trees.*

(*Walking to* **Joe**)  We hoped t'see you, Joe. (*Turning briefly to* **Anne**.)  Didn't we?

**Anne**  Yes. (*To* **John**.)  Come here to me this is men's talk.

**John** *goes to* **Anne** *and stands beside her.*

**Richard** (*standing beside* **Joe**)  Did the shoes fit you all right.

**Emma**  I've them 'ere, Mister Wheatley. I was carryin'um fo' 'im.

**Joe**  Thanks, Mister Wheatley.

**Anne** (*walking with* **John** *towards* **Emma**)  The snow is beautiful when the sun shines.

**Richard**  Have yer thought about the job?

**Emma**  'E needs more time t'think, Mister Wheatley.

**Anne** *and* **John** *stand near* **Emma**.

**Richard**  Joe can answer for 'imself. Joe?

**Joe** (*after a moment thinking*)  I'd like t'tekk it, Mister Wheatley –

**Richard**  That's settled then.

**Joe**  But –

**Richard**  But what?

**Joe**  I'm a fisherman.

**Richard**  We're all the same people, Joe.

**Anne**  If 'e doesn't want to, don't make 'im.

**Richard**  No, a want this sorted out. (*Looking* **Joe** *in the eye.*)
What've I done?

**Joe** *is silent.*

What 'aven't I given yer? Tell me'n I'll mekk it right.

**Joe** (*after a moment plucking up the courage*)  Will yer give us our land back, Mister Wheatley?

**Richard**  Aye, a thought that might be it. (*Even more harshly.*) And what mekks yer think it's your land?

**Joe**  'Cos we've a right to it.

**Richard**  What right is that?

**Joe**  My father's right, Mister Wheatley, that was his father's and should be mine. 'N' the fair justice that goes with it.

**Richard** *raises his hand to hit* **Joe** *across the face.*

**Anne** (*her voice rising*)  Leave 'im be, Richard.

**Richard**'s *hand stops momentarily and then it comes down powerfully, hitting* **Joe** *across the cheek and jaw.* **Joe** *doesn't resist, he falls to the ground.*

**Emma** *hides her eyes.* **John** *lets out a quiet shriek before closing his.* **Anne** *watches sadly.*

**Joe** (*picking himself up*)  An' if you don't give us it we're goyn t'tekk it.

**Emma**  Don't Joe.

**John** (*frightened*)  Don't, Dad.

**Anne**  Is that the way to treat someone?

**Richard**  Stay out of this, woman! (*Back to* **Joe**.) Yer think yer goyn t'tekk my land?

**Joe**  Aye.

**Richard** *raises his hand, he brings it down powerfully across* **Joe**'s *face.* **Joe** *falls to the ground again.*

(*Picking himself up. A small trickle of blood is running from the corner of his mouth*)  I'm weak, Mister Wheatley, not strong like you.

**Emma** *makes a dart towards* **Joe**. **Anne** *quickly grabs her hand and stops her.*

**Anne**  Don't girl.

**Richard** *raises his hand, he brings it down powerfully across* **Joe**'s *face.* **Joe** *falls to the ground.*

**John** What's 'e doin' it for? What's 'e done?

**Richard** *walks away from* **Joe** *and away from the other three.*

**Anne** *is still holding* **Emma**'s *hand.* **Anne** *lets her go.* **Emma** *rushes to* **Joe**.

**Emma** (*bending down beside him*) Joe.

**Joe** *is unconscious. Blood is coming from his mouth.*

**John** Is 'e dead?

**Emma** (*nursing him on her lap*) Joe.

**John** (*tugging at* **Anne**'s *sleeve*) Did yer hear me? Is 'e dead?

**Anne** I don't know, John.

**John** (*proudly*) He could fight anyone.

**Anne** Don't you ever fight, d'you hear?

**Richard** I don't know what came over me. Any learnin' yer do don't make yer less angry. I treat people fair. I'm a good man.

**Emma** You've killed 'im.

**Richard** *is looking at* **Anne**. **Anne** *is silent.*

**Richard** I know it's not the way your God behaves. (*After a moment's pause.*) I'll walk on my own back to the farm.

**Richard** *exits, quite slowly, through the gate and through the trees.*

**John** (*tugging at* **Anne**'s *sleeve*) Are we goyn too?

**Anne** In a minute. I want to help Emma first.

**Anne** *walks to* **Emma**.

**Emma** It's all right. I'll do it.

**Anne** (*taking* **Emma**'s *arm*) Come here, girl.

**Emma** *stands up and falls into* **Anne**'s *arms. She sobs.* **John** *watches.*
Sssh.

*A slight pause.*

**John** I'm goyn after him.

**Anne** Don't get lost now.

**John** *walks through the gate, as he exits through the trees he starts to run.*

*A slight pause.*

Sssh.

**Emma** *sobs more loudly.*

Eh, shush now, shush.

*The sunlight fades to blackout.*

## Scene Three

*Middlewood. The night of New Year's Eve.*

*A full moon is shining through the trees casting quite a bright light. There are one or two eerie shadows.*

**Emma**, *wearing the same clothes, is sitting alone on the tree trunk.*

**William Elderberry** *enters.*

**William** *is a dwarf in his early thirties. He has a kind, lively face and he speaks without a trace of an accent. He is dressed for the cold in shoes, stockings, breeches, shirt, waistcoat, neck-tie, and a top coat.*

**Emma** *sees him and stands up, she looks frightened.* **William** *stops.*

**William** Don't be frightened. I don't mean you harm.

**Emma** (*taking a step backwards*) A've bin waitin' fo'yer.

**William** (*mystified*) My name's William Elderberry. I'm with the fair.

**Emma** Where're your friends?

**William** (*pointing briefly behind him*) They're back along the road there. Our carvans are stuck in the deep snow. I was looking for someone to help us pull them out.

**Emma** I thought you lived in the ground.

**William** No. I realize it's late. We shouldn't have been on the road at this time, especially on New Year's Eve.

**Emma** Where yer goyn t'tekk me?

**William**  I don't understand.

**Emma** (*taking a step backwards*)  Now I've seen you, a'm scared. A thought a wouldn' be. You are a boggart, aren't you? Where're your horns?

**William** *feels the top of his head.*

**William** (*smiling*)  I don't have any. What are boggarts.

**Emma**  The little men who live in these woods. (*Taking a step backwards.*)  Yer horns must've dropped off, like cows, when you were fightin'.

**William**  I'm not a boggart.

**Emma**  Yer live in the roots o'trees, don' yer? 'N' tekk people away t'yer den?

**William**  Who told you this?

**Emma**  Folk've seen yer from the village.

**William**  D'you wish a boggart to take you?

**Emma** *nods.*

(*Taking a step towards her*)  I really am not a boggart.

**Emma** (*taking a step back*)  Boggarts are liars.

*They stop.*

**William**  Are you so unhappy? What's your name?

**Emma**  Emma. Emma Braye.

**William**  I am with the fair.

**William** *takes three balls from his pocket. He juggles with them.*

This is how I make my living.

**Emma** *watches blankly.* **William** *catches the balls and stops juggling.*

Come to me, Emma.

**Emma** (*staying tentatively*)  Do I 'ave t'do as you say?

**Emma** *walks to* **William**.

**William**  Feel the top of my head.

**Emma** *tentatively feels the top of* **William**'s *head.*

Are there any horns there?

**Emma**   No.

**Emma** *takes her hand away.* **William** *produces one of the balls from his mouth.*

'Ow did yer do that? D'you eat those?

**William** *puts out a hand to* **Emma**'s *ear.* **Emma** *jumps back.*

**William**   Don't move.

**William** *produces a ball from behind* **Emma**'s *ear. He coughs. Another ball drops from his mouth. He catches it.*

(*Smiling*) Mrs Elderberry taught me.

**Emma**   Who's Mrs Elderberry?

**William**   My wife.

**Emma**   Is she as small as you?

**William** (*brightly*) She's smaller than me. (*Putting the balls in his pocket.*) Won't you tell me what the matter is?

**Emma** *looks down, turns, and walks away a pace.*

(*Blowing into his hands. Brightly*) It's jolly, jolly cold here. Are there any men to help us move our caravans? (*Rubbing his hands.*) Mine's at a steep angle, I'd be rolling out of bed if I went to sleep.

*A slight pause.*

Please tell me.

*A slight pause.*

Let me consult Mrs Elderberry.

**William** *puts his hands to his temples and thinks for a moment.*

I think you've been in love, haven't you?

**Emma**   'Ow did you know?

**William**   Mrs Elderberry told me.

**Emma**   Yer can't do nowt. No one can. 'E's dead. The boggarts've taken 'is body.

**William**   Where have they taken it to?

**Emma** A don't know. We left it 'ere. When a came back it'd gone. A came back wi' the pony. It's all my fault. Joe was right. 'E would be alive if it weren't f'me.

**William** Don't distress yourself.

**Emma** I've 'ad enough.

*A slight pause.*

**William** You loved him very much, didn't you?

**Emma** *nods.*

**Emma** We were goyn t'the city. I were wrong, I stopped us. We were goyn t'go to York.

**William** York has a castle. We pitch our fair on the green nearby.

**Emma** What's it like?

**William** York is crowded with people. All seeking work like you and your – Joe?

**Emma** *nods.*

Like you and Joe would have been. The streets of York are littered with destitute men. The poverty and disease I've seen should be a crime. I much prefer the country. Thousands of people have gone to the cities. This is the place for you.

**Emma** *smiles slightly.*

**Emma** D'you travel a lot?

**William** All over Yorkshire. We're on our way from Scarborough. We should be in Whitby now for the New Year.

**Emma** I've never bin t'the fair.

**William** Haven't you?

**Emma** *smiles.*

You're beautiful when you smile.

**Emma** Yer jus' sayin' that.

**William** I understand why Joe loved you.

**Emma** (*surprised*) D'you think 'e did?

**William**  Yes.

**Emma**  I weren't sure. Especially after what I did. (*Feeling upset again.*) I wondered if yer stopped lovin' when you were dead. I want 'im still t'love me.

**William**  I've upset you again.

**Emma**  Yer haven't. (*Brighter.*) Yer not a boggart, are you?

**William**  (*smiling*)  I'm beginning to feel like one, the way you keep saying it.

**Emma**  I wonder where they are?

**William**  (*blowing into his hands*)  Wrapped up warm I imagine.

**Emma**  What happens at a fair?

**William**  (*going into his act*)  Jolly up, jolly up, step right this way, Ladies and Gentlemen. See the moving wax-works, the dancing horse, the impersonators. Tumblers, musicians, fire-eaters. Our troop of tight-rope dancing children. (*Bowing to her.*) Step right this way, my girl.

**Emma** *laughs.*

Come on, step this way.

**Emma** *walks past him.* **William** *does part of his act; he produces a long red handkerchief from the inside of his mouth.* **Emma** *watches.*

(*Bowing.*) Thank you. (*Looking up.*) People usually clap.

**Emma** *claps.*

Who's this?

**William** *impersonates George III.* **Emma** *looks blank.*

That's George the third, our King.

**William** *impersonates The Archbishop of York; he sticks his bum out and makes a loud farting noise.*

**Emma**  (*smiling*)  I don't know.

**William**  The Archbishop of York, farting.

**Emma**  I haven't seen them.

**William**  (*standing upright again*)  Haven't you seen pictures of them?

**Emma**  No.

**William**  They have in the towns. People like it when the Archbishop farts.

**Emma**  I know what he does.

**William**  You are a funny girl.

**William** *smiles. They look at one another for a moment.* **Emma** *looks down and walks away a pace.*

(*Brightly*)  I had better be going back really.

**Emma** (*turning to him*)  Don't go yet.

**William**  Mrs Elderberry will be wondering where I am.

**Emma**  I'd like to meet your wife.

**William**  Would you?

**Emma**  Yes.

**William**  Have you no hope?

**Emma** *shakes her head slightly.*

Another man will cross your path, won't he?

**Emma** (*sitting down on the log*)  It's not jus' Joe.

**William**  What is it then?

**Emma**  I can't live 'ere anymore.

**William**  Why?

**Emma** (*tentatively*)  Cos of what's 'appened. It's terrible. (*Looking at* **William**.) There was a big fight between us and the fishermen.

**William** (*sitting down beside her*)  I don't understand.

**Emma**  The fishermen came up t'take their land back. They fought in this field. (*Her voice rising.*) They must think I tol' Mister Wheatley, but I didn', 'e guessed. (*After a moment's pause.*) About thirty or forty fishermen came up from the Bay. All they were armed with were sticks. The farmers 'ad guns. When the fishermen tried t'pull down the fences, our farmers charged 'em. They were lyin' in wait. The fishermen 'ad no chance.

**William**  Go on?

**Emma**  In the end the fishermen jus' fled. Anywhere they could run where the snow weren't too deep. Out farmers were stronger'n chased 'em. Pockets o'men jus' fightin' wi' their bare fists. 'N' gun-shots ringin' out.

**William**  What happened?

**Emma**  One farmer was killed, one fisherman and another six fishermen caught. The rest of 'em got away.

**William** *looks down at the snow.*

The six that were caught were taken to the Justice.

**William** (*looking up*)  Oh dear.

**Emma**  The villagers raised a flag of victory in the village square. A couldn't stand the celebration of it. The fishermen're t'be taken t'York assizes. Mister Wheatley is travelling there tomorrow. He wants them all hanged to set an example.

**William**  Joe was a fisherman, was he?

**Emma** *nods.*

**Emma**  He weren't in the fight though. 'E were killed before.

*A slight pause.*

Joe would 'ave liked you an' all. What do I do? I 'ave t'live with Mister Wheatley.

**William**  Let me consult Mrs Elderberry.

**Emma**  D'you alwez do that?

**William** (*looking at* **Emma**)  Yes.

**William** *puts his hands to his temples and thinks for a moment.*

(*Brightly*)  Firstly, she says you musn't let the boggarts get you. Because Joe's not with them. Secondly, she says you must think about the future.

**Emma**  Is that all?

**William**  And have some hope.

**Emma**  Why?

**William** Because when you've lost hope, you've lost everything, haven't you?

**Emma** *looks down and thinks for a moment.*

**Emma** (*looking back up*) Is Mrs Elderberry dead?

**William** I was in love too.

**Emma** She is, isn't she?

**William** (*standing up*) I ought to be back to my caravan.

**Emma** Tell me. (*Looking up at him.*) It'll give me hope if she is.

**William** She died of the fever five years ago. (*He has heard something.*) Listen. What's that?

*They listen.*

*A church clock can be heard chiming faintly from the distance.*

It's New Year's Eve. It must be midnight. A drink.

**William** *produces two small glasses from his pocket.*

**Emma** Where did yer get those from?

**William** (*giving them to her*) You hold them please.

**Emma** *holds the glasses.* **William** *produces a small bottle of wine. He pours wine into the glasses and puts the bottle away.*

*The clock is striking midnight.*

**William** *takes one glass from* **Emma.**

To the New Year.

**Emma** (*standing up*) To the New Year.

*They drink and empty their glasses.*

**William** If you could send some men in the morning I'd be grateful.

**Emma** I will.

**William** Look after yourself.

**Emma** I'll try to.

**William** *turns and exits towards his caravan.*

(*Calling after him. Holding the glass at arm's length.*) You've forgotten your glass.

*A slight pause.*

Good luck, William Elderberry.

**Emma** *stands holding the empty glass.*

*The moonlight fades to blackout.*

# Act Three

## Scene One

**Anne Wheatley**'s *kitchen at Middlewood farm. Twenty years later. The evening of July the 11th. 1797.*

*The light from a full moon is shining through the window.*

**Anne** *is sitting on the bench at the table. Beside her is an ink-pot, and with a quill she is writing her diary in her notebook. A candle nearby is giving quite a lot of light.*

*The cupboard in the dresser where she keeps her notebooks is open. A rush-light is burning on the dresser itself. The outside door is not bolted, the bar of wood is resting against the frame.*

**Anne** *is wearing the gown, she has the woollen shawl across her shoulders. She writes slowly and purposefully, thinking about every sentence.*

*An owl hoots outside.*

**Anne** *blows on the ink to dry it. She turns the page and writes another line.*

*There is a muffled knock on the outside door.*

**Anne** *looks up.*

*A short silence.*

**Anne** *writes.*

*The knock again, this time louder.*

**Anne** (*standing up, going to the door*) Who's there?

*A short silence.*

It's late. Who is it? (*After a moment's pause.*) Is it you again, boy?

*A short silence.*

I'm not opening the door until you say who you are.

*The knock again.*

I should warn you I've a dog beside me.

**Anne** *slowly opens the door.*

**Joe** *is standing there. He is dressed in his best clothes; shoes, stockings, breeches, waistcoat, shirt, neck-tie, and a jacket.*

**Joe**　Mrs Wheatley?

**Anne**　(*she doesn't recognize him. Suspiciously*)　Yes?

**Joe**　Do you remember me?

**Anne**　No. Who are you? What d'you want at this time of night?

**Joe**　You don't recognize me?

**Anne**　No.

**Joe**　I'm Joe Waterman, Mrs Wheatley.

**Anne** *looks at* **Joe**, *she takes a step back from the door.*

**Anne**　I don't know who you are, but go please.

**Joe** *takes a step into the kitchen.*

**Joe**　I haven't come here to frighten you, Mistress.

**Anne**　(*stammering*)　Joe Waterman, but you're dead.

**Joe**　I was left for dead twenty years ago.

**Anne**　(*sharply*)　Go away from here. What d'you want?

**Joe**　I've come for your help.

**Anne**　Help! How can we help you?

*A short silence.*

**Joe**　Emma mentioned t'me once about a Frenchman who came here.

**Anne**　(*still quite sharply*)　What of it?

**Joe**　I wondered what he looked like, Mistress?

**Anne**　Who?

**Joe**　The Frenchman who came.

**Anne**　Why?

**Joe**　(*slightly hesitantly*)　We think we've a Frenchman at Bay Town.

**Anne** *goes white. She walks to the rocking-chair.*

**Joe**  I beg of you, Mrs Wheatley.

**Anne**  Go. Please go.

**Anne** *sits in the chair.* **Joe** *shuffles nervously, he stays.*

Why did you come here? If it is you, Joe.

**Joe**  I had t'come now. It will be too late tomorrow.

**Anne** (*softly*)  How could I ever forget you.

**Anne** *closes her eyes, she rocks in the chair.*

*A slight pause.*

**Joe**  If you'd jus' tell me what the Frenchman looked like.

**Anne**  Emma said you were alive. We didn't believe her.

**Joe**  Do you remember?

**Anne** (*opening her eyes*)  The Frenchman? Yes, I do. He was an older man. Squire Boulby brought him to Richard. He was here to learn the new farming, he kept slipping in the snow.

**Joe**  Was he covered in hair?

**Anne**  He was bald.

**Joe**  A'yer sure?

**Anne**  Why?

**Joe**  The Frenchman we have is covered in hair. A boat was wrecked las' night –

**Anne**  We know.

**Joe**  Oh?

**Anne**  We watch you, Joe.

**Joe** (*getting over his surprise*)  Well, we reckon 'e's from that. But I think he's an animal. Did your Frenchman walk upright?

**Anne**  Yes.

**Joe**  Ours walks on his hands and knees.

**Anne**  He was like you or me. He spoke slightly different, with an accent.

**Joe** Ours grunts'n groans, 'n' shrieks now'n again. Yet he looks human. Sometimes, anyway. He has this way of lookin' at yer. 'N' 'e's strong like a man. The town's in panic.

**Anne** Where is he?

**Joe** We have him in a cage. (*After a moment's pause.*) He's not a Frenchman, Mistress. We're being made t'look so stupid.

**Anne** (*after a moment's pause*) Is that why you came?

**Joe** (*after nodding once*) T'be certain.

**Anne** It must've taken courage?

**Joe** I waited 'till dark, so no one would see me.

*A slight pause.*

Thank you.

**Joe** *turns and walks towards the open door.*

**Anne** (*standing up*) Don't go, stay.

**Joe** (*turning, by the door*) The whole town is watchin'. I should be there myself.

**Anne** *walks to* **Joe**, *she feels his arms.*

**Anne** You are real, aren't you.

**Joe** (*hesitantly*) I don't know what we've got t'say to each other, Mrs Wheatley.

**Anne** It is you, Joe.

**Joe** *looks embarrassed, he shuffles.*

Will you stay?

**Joe** A few moments.

**Anne** *walks to the door, she closes it.* **Joe** *walks into the kitchen. They turn and look at one another.*

What happened to Emma?

**Anne** She died, Joe, giving birth to her child.

**Joe** A waited for her, but she never came. A waited, for a year a waited. Then a stole up one night an' found her stone in the graveyard.

**Anne**  The girl'd whittled away t'nothing out of grief f'you.

**Joe**  What happened to the child?

**Anne**  She's upstairs. Asleep I hope.

*A slight pause.*

**Joe**  That's quite a shock. That I didn't know.

**Anne**  I brought her up.

**Joe**  Is she like her mother at all?

**Anne** (*after thinking for a moment*)  I'm not very good at comparing people. Yes, I think they are. They've the same spirit.

**Joe** (*after a moment's pause*)  Does she know about me?

**Anne**  I've tried to tell her. In my own way. Recently I've tried.

**Joe** *turns, he walks one pace. He stops and looks at* **Anne.**

I'm getting older, Joe. I won't be here for very much longer. I didn't want to go without her knowing.

*A slight pause.*

And it's time she was married an' knew the truth. She'll marry well, she'll make a good wife.

*A slight pause.*

All these years I've written a diary. Just my thoughts, the day t'day things. I discovered they were being moved. I let her go on with it.

**Joe**  Why didn't you tell'er when she was little.

**Anne**  How could I, Joe? Would you have done? The spite in the village, they wouldn't have let the child live.

**Joe**  No.

**Anne**  I wanted to tell her.

*A slight pause.*

But it takes courage after so long.

**Joe** *turns, he walks the one pace back. He stops and looks at* **Anne.**

**Joe**  I should be goyn.

**Anne** We're not strangers, Joe.

**Joe** I don't know why a came. A shouldn't o'come.

*The upstairs door slowly opens.* **Betsy** *peers round, she has a candle.*

**Betsy** I've been listening at the door.

**Betsy** *steps into the kitchen. She is wearing the white nightdress.*

Is that my father?

**Anne** (*angrily*) Back to bed this instant.

**Betsy** No, Aunt, I'm not a child.

**Joe** *is staring at* **Betsy.**

(*To* **Joe**) Are you my father?

**Anne** (*huffily*) Don't be silly, girl.

**Betsy** Please, Aunt.

**Anne** Of course he's not your father.

**Betsy** (*turning to* **Anne.** *Her voice rising*) Why're you denyin' him?

**Betsy** *looks at* **Joe.**

Are you my father?

**Joe** *looks at* **Anne.**
*A slight pause.* **Anne** *and* **Joe** *look away from one another.*

(*Looking between them*) Why're you both quiet? I know. I could tell from the conversation. What do it matter?

*A short silence.*

(*Relaxed, friendly*) I've of'en tried to picture you. Yer not at all like I imagined.

**Betsy** *walks to the table. She puts the candle down.*

(*To* **Joe**) The Mistress alwez told me I was her sister's child.

**Anne** (*calmly*) You've seen now, back to bed.

**Betsy** Why can't you talk about it, Aunt?

**Anne** Mister Waterman was going, we're keeping him here.

**Betsy** Were you?

**Joe** (*shyly*)  I was goyn, yes.

**Betsy** *walks to the outside door and stands in front of it.*

**Betsy** (*to* **Anne**)  Why don't we have that talk now?

*A short silence.* **Betsy** *looks between* **Anne** *and* **Joe**

**Joe**  Yer should praise yer Aunt f'what shiz done.

**Betsy**  Will yer tell me about you?

**Joe** *looks at* **Anne** *and then back to* **Betsy**.

**Joe**  It was your mother really who taught me everything I know. (*To* **Anne**.) D'you mind if I sit down?

**Anne**  No. Do.

**Joe** *sits down on the bench.* **Anne** *walks to the rocking-chair and sits down.*

**Joe**  We were goyn to marry, an' then that bad winter came. (*To* **Anne**.) Didn' it?

**Anne**  Yes.

**Betsy**  All that is in the diary.

**Anne**  Come away from the door, child, the draught will give you a chill.

**Betsy** *walks to the bench and sits down.*

**Joe**  At that time I worked with my father and three brothers. We had the one cobble. We starved.

**Betsy**  I know about the fences.

**Joe**  After the battle, all we decided we could do, was to become fishermen proper. With more boats. 'N' store food f'the winter. We'd been farmers y'see, as well. (*To* **Anne**.) Hadn't we?

**Anne** *nods.*

We cut down trees, stolen off the farm land. An' built cobbles. (*Looking at* **Anne**.) We're still poor, but we're better than we were.

**Betsy**  What about you?

**Joe**  I've jus' sold my cobble.

**Betsy**  What for?

**Joe** (*slightly tentatively*)  I'm hoping to open a school.

**Betsy**  Someone told me that.

**Joe** *looks sympathetically at* **Betsy**. *He smiles.*

**Joe**  For the children of the town. Teach them t'read'n write.

**Anne**  How will you make a living?

**Joe**  The towners who send children will have to pay me. It'll be a struggle because we've a new preacher at the town. A methodist. I dislike their preachin', they think children should work. He's made them suspicious. A few have promised to help. Enough to begin with. (*Proudly.*) It'll be the first school at Bay Town.

**Betsy** (*smiling*)  They'll come.

**Joe** (*smiling at* **Betsy**)  I hope so.

**Anne**  I wish we had a school at Fylingthorpe.

**Joe** (*looking at* **Anne**)  School is a new idea t'the likes of us. It'll take gettin' used to.

**Anne**  All the new ideas are like that.

**Joe**  I think so.

*A short silence.* **Anne** *and* **Joe** *quickly feel embarrassed, they look away from one another.*

**Betsy**  Am I like you imagined?

**Anne**  Don't pester Mister Waterman, Betsy.

**Joe**  It's alright. (*To* **Betsy**.) I don't reckon you are because I didn't know you see. I didn't know what had happened. I didn't know there was a you. I've wondered.

**Betsy** (*brightly*)  I wondered all the time.

**Joe** *smiles.*

**Anne**  Have you married?

**Joe**  No, unfortunately.

**Anne**  Why not?

**Joe**  It didn't seem right to.

**Betsy**  D'you know a fisherman called Andrew Cove?

**Joe** Yes, I do. Thomas Cove's son.

**Betsy** *plucks up her courage and stands up.*

**Betsy** I want t'tell yer both something.

**Anne** (*closing her eyes*) Don't, Betsy.

**Anne** *rocks in the chair.*

**Betsy** (*looking at* **Anne**) Tim Appleyard were right.

**Anne** I don't want to hear, child.

**Betsy** *looks at* **Joe**.

**Betsy** I've bin meetin' Andrew Cove. We're goyn t'get married one day.

**Anne** *stops rocking and opens her eyes.*

**Anne** (*her voice rising*) Get out of this house!

**Betsy** (*turning to* **Anne**) Yer knew, didn't yer?

**Anne** (*angrily*) Of course I didn't know.

**Betsy** (*tapping the side of her head*) Yer can keep things up here. But as soon as the' said, yer can't talk any more. Why?

**Anne** *closes her eyes and rocks in the chair. A slight pause.*

(*To* **Joe**) I met 'im in the woods. I was pickin' mushrooms one day. He were poachin' rabbits.

**Joe** *looks down.*

(*To* **Anne**, *calmly*) It's you who believe the fishermen 'ave two 'eads. Not me. Yer can't stand up f'the truth.

**Anne** (*opening her eyes. Harshly*) Tim Appleyard was too convincing.

**Betsy** A bet 'e were. Idle layabout.

**Anne** I don't want to hear it.

**Anne** *closes his eyes.*

I'll have to apologize to him. He was roundly scolded.

*A slight pause.*

**Betsy** D'yer want me t'go, Aunt? If yer want me to, a will.

**Anne** (*eyes closed, calmly*)  You're a disappointment to me.

**Betsy** (*sympathetically*)  A can't do much about that, a'm sorry.

*A slight pause.*

D'yer want me t'go?

**Anne** (*opening her eyes*)  Why did you do it, Betsy? Why have you ruined everything?

**Betsy**  I haven't.

**Anne**  But you have. You could've been such a good girl.

**Betsy**  No, Aunt.

*A slight pause.*

I understand what my mother felt. I'm goyn t'do what she should have done.

**Betsy** *walks to the upstairs door and goes out leaving the door open.*

**Anne**  What a terrible mess.

**Anne** *closes her eyes, she rocks in the chair.*

*Silence for a moment.*

**Joe**  Did you know, Mistress?

**Anne** (*opening her eyes*)  I guessed.

**Joe**  Then what do it matter?

**Anne**  Does it not bother you?

**Joe**  I've wanted t'come here f'a long time.

**Anne**  Have you told anyone?

**Joe**  No. (*Looking down slightly.*) I admit that. (*Looking back up.*) We could start, Mrs Wheatley?

*The owl hoots outside.*

**Anne**  I'm not an intelligent woman, Joe. I've alwez lost the things I treasured most. My husband. Emma. My son. And now it seems I'm to lose Betsy.

**Joe** (*after thinking for a moment*)  We've lost them because of conflict, Mistress.

**Anne** *is thinking.*

**Anne**  Things seem to repeat themselves. As spring and sowing, follows autumn and ploughing.

**Joe**  We can change that. Stop that. (*After a moment's pause.*) Emma was right all those years ago. It's no good running away. The city wouldn't've been f'us.

*A slight pause.*

(*Smiling*) She's beautiful.

**Anne**  Who?

**Joe**  Betsy.

**Anne** (*proudly*)  Is she?

**Joe**  She does remind me of Emma. In my mind Emma is still as young. (*After a moment's pause.*) I meant what I said about praisin' yer, Mistress.

**Anne**  You're a better man than me, Joe.

**Joe** *sits back.*

What is this boy like?

**Joe**  Andrew Cove? Don't you remember his father?

**Anne**  No.

**Joe**  His father was one of my pals. He was one of those hanged.

**Anne**'s *gaze drops to the floor.*

Andrew 'imself is a bright lad.

**Anne** (*her gaze coming back to* **Joe**)  D'you think they'll have talked together?

**Joe** (*shrugging*)  Wouldn't you 'ave done?

**Anne**  I wonder what they've said about me.

**Joe**  He's not the cheeky sort.

**Anne**  What does he do?

**Joe**  'E fishes a cobble with Edward Tideswell.

**Anne**  How old is he?

**Joe**  He's about twenty.

**Anne**  And he's bright, you say?

**Joe**  He's a sense of good fun, Mistress.

**Anne**  I'm glad. I was trying to picture him.

*A slight pause.*

What d'you think I should do?

**Betsy** *enters through the open upstairs door. She has dressed hastily in shoes, a gown, and a red cloak. The bonnet on her head is crooked. She is carrying a canvas bag.*

**Anne** *stands up.*

(*Brightly*)  Here she is.

**Betsy** *stands in the middle of the kitchen and puts her bag down.*

**Betsy**  I'll go then, Aunt.

**Anne** *looks at* **Joe**. **Joe** *stands up.*

I don't know why you came but thank you, Mister Waterman.

**Anne**  Won't you wait until morning?

**Betsy**  No.

*A slight pause.*

**Anne** (*walking to* **Betsy**)  Your bonnet's crooked. Untie it, let me set it straight.

**Betsy** *unties the bonnet.* **Anne** *puts it straight on* **Betsy**'s *head. She starts to tie the ribbon.*

I see you've taken my bag.

**Betsy**  I don't have one of my own.

*The ribbon is fastened.* **Betsy** *picks up the bag and walks to the outside door.*

**Anne**  Please don't, Betsy. At least wait until it's light.

**Betsy** *opens the door.*

**Betsy** (*turning to* **Anne**)  If I wait, I'll never go. (*After a moment's pause.*) Thank you for all you've done.

**Betsy** *goes out. She closes the door slowly behind her.*

*A short silence.*

**Anne**  Will she ever come back, d'you think?

**Joe**  I don't know.

**Anne**  Half an hour ago everything was all right.

**Anne** *walks to the window and looks out.*

**Joe**  I should really go with her, Mrs Wheatley. If they see 'er 'n' realise where shiz from –

**Anne** (*turning from the window. Her voice rising*)  Why didn't you stop her then?

**Joe** (*quite quietly*)  I couldn't have stopped 'er.

**Anne** (*angrily*)  What if they stone her, Mister Waterman?

**Joe** (*calmly*)  It would be no worse than what you did to us.

**Anne**  But she's your daughter.

**Joe**  She might've been my daughter twenty years ago.

**Anne**  How can you stand there and say that?

**Joe**  Because it's what I think.

**Anne**  So you'd let them stone your daughter?

**Joe**  If Andrew Cove came here, would you stone him?

*Silence for a moment.*

**Anne**  No, I'd try'n stop them.

**Joe**  Then I will try'n do the same.

*A slight pause.*

I'm listened to at Bay Town. It's for the best.

*The outside door opens.* **John** *enters. He is drunk.*

**John** (*seeing* **Anne**)  Where's Betsy? (*Closing the door.*)  I got Harriet Woodforde drunk'n she danced with me. (*Looking at* **Joe**.)  Chris Smith played 'is fiddle. Who's he?

**Joe** *looks at* **Anne**. *Silence for a moment.*

(*To* **Anne**, *angrily*)  Who's he? Who's that in my house?

*A moment's pause.*

(*Lurching forward towards* **Anne**) Tell me, woman!

**Anne** It's Mister Waterman.

**John** (*looking at* **Joe**) Mister Waterman who?

**Anne** Mister Waterman from Bay Town.

**John** If he's a fisherman, hang 'im!

**John** *lurches forward towards* **Joe** *with his fists clenched.* **Joe** *moves out of the way.* **John** *falls to the ground.*

(*Picking himself up*) I don't know a Mister Waterman.

**Anne** You're drunk.

**John** Of course a'm drunk. The whole of New Plough Inn were drunk. I paid for 'em. They like me now. (*Pointing a finger at* **Anne**.) You don't mean anythin' to 'em any more.

**John** *hangs his head.*

**Joe** I'll go, Mrs Wheatley.

**John** (*looking up. Pointing his finger at* **Joe**) I remember you. You're dead. (*Turning incredulously to his mother.*) He's dead, Ma.

**John** *collapses in a heap on the stone floor.* **Joe** *walks to the outside door.*

**Anne** (*walking to the door*) Will you bring me news of Betsy.

**Joe** I'll try.

**Anne** *opens the door.* **Joe** *is looking at* **John**.

**Anne** Don't worry about him, I can manage sufficiently well.

**Anne** *and* **Joe** *look at one another.*

**Joe** Goodnight then, Mistress.

**Anne** Goodnight, Joe.

**Joe** *exits.* **Anne** *slowly closes the door.* **John** *picks himself up.*

**John** I remember Joe Waterman. (*Blinking.*) Where's he gone? Where's the ghost?

**Anne** *is looking at him.*

(*Looking round the kitchen*) A mus' be dreaming. (*Looking at* **Anne**.) Yer can't hang a ghost. What're yer lookin' at me for?

(*Angrily.*) Stop lookin' at me!

**John** *straightens up, he tries to be sober.*

Joe Waterman's come back to haunt us. I'm drunk. You should get drunk.

**Anne** (*tenderly*) Is this your answer to everything, John?

**John** *stumbles backwards towards the table. He props himself up on it.*

**John** Don't treat me like a little boy. I'm not a little boy.

**John** *sees the notebook. He looks at* **Anne**. *He pulls the notebook towards him.*

Betsy's been reading these you know.

**Anne** Don't touch them please.

**John** All the lies in here, she believes.

**John** *looks at the notebook.*

**Anne** Leave them, John.

**John** All the lies about my father. (*Looking again.*) What've you put for t'day.

**Anne** (*walking to him*) I asked you to leave them.

**John** (*pushing her away, quite roughly*) Ge' off.

**Anne** (*after regaining her composure*) Is this the way to treat your mother?

**John** I'm a new an' different man.

**John** *picks up the diary.*

**Anne** (*going to him*) Don't John, please.

**John** (*pushing her away, roughly*) Ge'off!

**Anne** *falls to the floor.* **John** *rips the notebook in half.*

That's what I think about you an' your lies.

**John** *throws the two halves of the notebook towards* **Anne**. **Anne** *picks them up, her hair has fallen out of place, she stands up.* **John** *collapses down, he sits on the bench.*

Why d'you hate me, Ma?

**Anne** *is close to tears. She says nothing. She pushes her hair back into place.*

That was naughty, weren't it?

**Anne** *walks to the table.*

Why don't you love me?

**Anne** *puts the two halves of the notebook down.*

**Anne**   I do love you.

**John**   Why didn't you love my father?

**Anne**   I loved him too.

**Anne** *sits down on the bench.*

I loved him with all my heart. When he died, I died.

*A slight pause.*

**John**   It's you who's made me like this.

*A slight pause.*

A didn' mean t'rip yer diary.

*A slight pause.*

Where're the others?

**Anne**   In the cupboard.

**John**   A didn't rip them. I'll glue it back together. (*Reaching behind him.*) Where is it?

**Anne**   Leave it now.

**John** *stops. A slight pause.*

**John**   Did my father love you?

**Anne**   (*after a moment's pause*)  No, I don't think he did.

**John**   I'm like 'im, aren't I? That's what you didn't want. 'N' yet you loved him.

*A slight pause.*

I loved 'im as well. He was the apple of my eye.

**Anne**   I loved him, but I hated what he did.

**John**   Jus' like yer hate me? F'being like 'im.

**Anne** (*after a moment's pause*)  Yes.

*A slight pause.*

We should've talked a long time ago.

*The owl hoots outside.*

**John** (*imitating it*)  Twit-twoo.

*A slight pause.*

I think I'm very drunk.

*The two candles and the rushlight are burning.*


## Scene Two

*The beach and town at Robin Hood's Bay. A few moments later.*

*Sand. The house of **Robert** and **Molly Storm**. Grass. Standing on the grass is **Robert**'s clinker-built fishing cobble. The cobble is called 'Molly', it is painted on in rough white lettering. Near the house, on the sand, is an old cart. On top of the cart is a wooden cage.*

*The light from a full moon is shining.*

*A gentle sea can be heard lapping against the shore.*

**Stockton** *and **Mary** are inside the cage. They are still.*

**Robert** *is sitting on a bench a short distance from the cage. He has the musket beside him. He is smoking a clay pipe.*

**Mary** *talks to **Stockton**.*

**Mary**  Me brother were the Skip-Jack, turning the jack on our Master's skip-roastin' fire. A were the scullery maid. 'E didn't treat us proper. One day 'e were beatin' me brother, so me brother pushed him in the fire. All 'is clothes set alight. We ran off f'fear what 'e'd do to us.

**Molly** *appears from the house carrying two tankards of ale. She walks down towards **Robert**.*

**Robert**  You go to bed, Love.

**Molly**  I'll 'ave one with yer.

**Mary** (*watching them*)  I still 'aven' 'ad that drink, Mistress.

**Molly**  You be quiet, boy.

**Mary** (*standing up*)  A'm a girl, a've told yer.

**Robert** (*standing up. His voice booming towards* **Mary**)  Eh, you be quiet, an' don't be cheeky.

**Molly** *gives one tankard to* **Robert**.

Ta, thank you. (*Sitting down.*) If my boys were as cheeky as 'im, a'd thrash them.

**Mary**  Yer daren't come near me, dare yer? Yer frightened.

**Robert** *stands up.*

**Molly**  Leave 'im be.

**Robert** *sits down.*

**Mary**  Told yer.

**Molly** *sits down beside him.*

**Robert** (*his voice booming to* **Mary**)  Yer'll be 'angin' by mornin' you boy.

**Mary**  A won't.

**Molly** *drinks.* **Stockton** *stands up, he walks round in a circle.*

You'll be 'angin' by evenin'.

**Robert** *drinks.* **Stockton** *sits down again.*

Wait till our friends get 'ere.

**Molly** (*calling to* **Mary**)  Thess a few people tryin' t'sleep in this town.

**Peter Storm** *appears at the door of the house. He looks tired.*

**Peter** *is twelve years old. He is wearing a nightshirt.*

**Robert** (*his voice booming, but now softly, affectionately*)  What d'you want, Peter?

**Peter**  A'm frightened.

**Robert**  Yer should be in bed, tucked up.

**Molly**  Let 'im come down 'ere, 'e won't hurt.

**Peter** *walks towards them.*

'Re yer brothers asleep?

**Peter**  Yes, Mam. Tom's snorin'.

**Robert** (*affectionately*)  A boy of mine frightened, Peter?

**Molly**  Sit down. D'yer want a drop o' this?

**Peter** *sits down on the sand near the bench. He takes the tankard from* **Molly**. *He drinks half of it.*

**Peter**  I kept 'avin' bad dreams.

**Peter** *drinks the other half.*

**Molly**  A said a drop, not all of it.

**Peter** (*giving the tankard to his mother*)  Ta. Mam.

**Molly** *holds the tankard upside down. It is empty.*

**Robert**  Do 'e alwez drink like that?

**Mary**  Is 'e your boy?

**Peter**  A were thirsty.

**Molly**  I'll 'ave 'alf o'yours.

**Robert**  See what trouble yer cause by yer drinkin'.

**Robert** *pours half of his ale into* **Molly**'s *tankard.*

**Molly**  Peter's my favourite. 'E'll soon be a man. It's time 'e learnt t'hold 'is ale.

**Robert**  Yer alwez sayin' drink is ruinous?

**Molly**  So it is, too much of it.

**Robert** *drinks.*

**Robert**  I understand 'im bein' frightened, a small'n like 'im. 'E's far from a man. I'd 'ave bad dreams mesell.

**Mary**  Why do 'e get a drink?

**Robert** (*to* **Mary**)  I've warned you, boy.

**Peter** *looks at the cage, and then at his father.*

**Peter**  Where're the other Frenchmen, Dad?

**Robert**  If a knew that, Peter, a'd be fightin' 'em. Yer can feel safe.

**Peter**  A were dreamin' they chopped our heads off.

**Mary** (*still standing watching them*)  The' will do.

**Robert** (*his voice booming to* **Mary**)  We're Yorkshire folk. No Frenchman's gonna do that.

**Peter**  A'yer sure?

**Peter** *stretches out on the sand*.

**Robert**  'E ought t'be in 'is bed.

**Molly**  Let 'im be. Thess summat special about t'night.

**Robert** (*suspiciously*)  What d'yer mean, Molly?

**Molly**  Thess summat Christmas.

**Robert**  A don't reckon the' is.

**Molly**  Thess a ringle in the air. 'Aven't yer felt it?

**Robert**  I 'aven't.

**Molly**  A celebration.

**Robert**  I believe they're about us, Molly.

**Peter** *curls up into a ball*.

A d'feel proud though, bein' the one set to guard 'im.

**Molly** *smiles*.

**Molly**  I feel good t'night. It's a victory, ain' it?

**Robert**  Yer might learn t'rue those words.

**Peter** *closes his eyes*. **Molly** *moves closer to* **Robert**.

A bit o'love makin' an' all, is it? Yer've not got another one on the way?

**Molly** (*smiling*)  No.

**Robert**  I've bin thinkin', Molly. A don't think swallowin' them ten worms does any good.

**Molly** *cuddles* **Robert**.

Not in front of the boy. Remember what Mister Wesley said.

**Molly** *stops*.

**Molly**  D'yer mean it?

**Robert** (*adamantly*) Aye, a do. I'm not 'avin' that. Supposin' that new Preacher Man were seein' us?

**Molly** 'E's not 'ere, 'e's in Scarborough.

**Robert** Aye, well it mekks n'difference.

**Molly** D'yer like 'im?

**Robert** He's a man of my heart.

**Molly** *looks at* **Robert**.

It's no use sayin' owt, a've decided.

**Mary** *sits down in the cage.* **Stockton** *stands up, he walks round on all fours in a circle.*

**Molly** (*tenderly*) Look at the boy, 'e's gone t'sleep.

**Robert** (*calling softly*) Peter?

*A slight pause.*

'E'as an' all. Fallin' t'sleep on the sand. Shall a pick 'im up'n tuck 'im in?

**Molly** Leave 'im. It's warm t'night.

**Robert** (*smiling*) The sky as 'is blanket.

**Stockton** *sits down. He settles, he is still.*

**Molly** A want Peter t'go t'Joe's school.

**Robert** We've 'ad this before, Molly.

**Molly** He's a delicate lad.

**Robert** Yer spoil 'im wi' too much affection.

**Molly** Mebbe a do, Robert.

**Robert** (*suspiciously*) What's that mean?

**Molly** Agreein' wi' yer.

**Robert** Why?

**Molly** *puts her fingers on* **Robert**'s *knee, she 'walks' them up his leg.*

**Molly** A won't rest till Peter's at that school.

**Robert** Where yer tekkin' them fingers?

**Robert** *watches.* **Molly** *continues.*

I'll 'ave t'go'n dig up worms in a minute.

**Molly** *stops.* **Stockton** *lets out a loud shriek.* **Molly** *and* **Robert** *jump. They look at the cage.*

I don't like it when 'e does that.

**Peter** *stirs. He changes position in his sleep.*
**Molly** *and* **Robert** *look at him.*

**Molly**  'E's 'avin' bad dreams again.

**Peter** *stops, he is still.*

**Robert**  I'd like t'read'n write.

**Molly**  Would yer?

**Robert**  Aye, a would. Be like some o'them farmers. Be like Joe.

**Betsy** *enters from the direction of Bay Ness. She is carrying the bag. She starts to cross quietly in front of the house.*

It ain't to be.

**Molly**  Wouldn't you like yer son to?

**Robert**  Aye, a would. It'd mekk me proud.

**Robert** *turns slightly towards the house.* **Betsy** *stops, hides in a shadow.*

(*Looking back to* **Molly**) 'E'd be a proper Gentelman, wouldn' 'e?

**Molly** *smiles.* **Betsy** *continues on her way.*

Yer need breedin' t'read'n write, it's not f'us, Molly.

**Betsy** *exits towards the town.*
**Robert** *turns to the house.*

Did you 'ear summat jus' then?

**Molly**  No.

**Robert**  Must 'ave imagined it. Me ears're workin' too well.

**Stockton** *lets out a loud shriek.*

(*Calling to the cage*)  Quiet, Frenchman.

**Peter** *stirs. He is still again.*

**Molly**  Yer get breedin' by learnin' t'read'n write.

**Robert**  Yer born with breedin', woman.

**Molly**  Joe Waterman weren't.

**Robert**  A like Joe, 'e's my friend, but 'e don't know it all.

**Molly**  Who d'folk turn to?

**Robert**  The' turn t'Joe. (*After a momen't pause.*) 'E's a fanciful man, woman.

**Moly**  Yer a strange'n, Robert Storm.

**Robert**  A'm a fisherman. A were born t'fish. A can see mesell now, Molly. A can see me place. Wi' me own cobble. A'm in charge o'mesell at last.

*A slight pause.*

Young Peter by me side. Young Thomas, young James, young Ned. Young Robin when 'e's back from the war.

**Molly** *smiles.*

All of us out there on the shiny sea.

**Molly** *looks at the sea.*

**Molly**  It's calm t'night.

**Robert**  Aye. As it should be.

**Molly** (*looking at* **Robert**)  Better than las' night?

**Robert** *nods.* **Mary** *stands up in the cage.*

**Mary** (*politely*)  Can I 'ave some food?

**Robert**  Ignore 'im, Molly.

**Mary**  I'm hungry. (*After a moment's pause.*) What yer goyn t'do with us?

**Robert**  Not up t'me, boy.

**Mary**  I saw a hangin' once, at the market town of Guisborough.

*A slight pause.*

**Mary** *sits down again.*

I don't like 'em, Stockton, d'you?

**Stockton** *is still.*

**Robert** (*looking at* **Peter**) Tekk the boy t'bed.

**Molly** *stands up. She stoops down.*

**Molly** (*tapping him on the shoulder*) Peter. Peter.

**Peter** *stirs and groans.*

Peter. Wake up.

**Peter** *opens his eyes.*

Stand up, Love, yer can't sleep there.

**Peter** *slowly stands up. He groans.*

**Robert** You go yersell an'all, if yer like.

**Molly** A'll come back.

**Molly** *puts an arm round* **Peter**'s *shoulder, they walk towards the house.*

**Joe** *enters from Bay Ness.*

(*Calling to* **Robert**) Joe's here.

**Molly** *stops with* **Peter**. **Robert** *sees* **Joe** *and stands up.*

**Robert** Yer dressed in yer finery?

**Joe** I've bin goyn round the watches, checkin' the men.

**Robert** Seen anythin'?

**Joe** Nothin'. Anything here?

**Robert** No. The boy natters on like a woman.

**Molly** Yer reckon we're safe, Joe?

**Joe** Yes. I want to have words.

**Robert** Speak yer mind.

**Joe** Where are they?

**Robert** Who?

**Joe**  The French soldiers.

**Robert**  In the caves'n woods.

**Joe**  We've searched the woods an' caves.

**Robert** *looks at* **Molly**.

(*Looking between them*) We haven't seen them because there aren't any. He's not a Frenchman.

**Robert** (*incredulously, his voice booming*)  Not a Frenchman?

**Robert** *looks at the cage.*

**Joe**  He's an animal. I said so when we first saw him.

**Robert**  I aint seen an animal like that?

**Joe**  Neither've I.

**Robert** *thinks for a moment.*

**Robert**  No, Joe, yer wrong this time. I ain' a cruel man but they deserve t'hang.

**Mary** *stands up, she watches them.*

**Joe** (*looking ay her*)  Molly?

**Robert**  She's my wife, she don't say nowt.

**Molly**  In any case I agree with 'im.

**Peter**  I know he's a Frenchman.

**Joe**  Eh?

**Peter**  I know he's a Frenchman.

**Joe**  D'yer? How?

**Peter**  Me Dad said so.

**Robert**  See, even the lad knows.

*A slight pause.*

**Joe**  I'm jus' sayin' what a think.

**Robert** (*sitting down*)  A like yer, Joe, but sometimes yer stupid. Despite yer learnin' from all them books.

**Joe** (*looking at* **Robert**)  Aye.

*A slight pause.*

**Molly**  I'll say goodnight.

**Joe**  Goodnight, Molly.

**Molly** *exits with* **Peter** *into the house.* **Robert** *and* **Joe** *look at one another.* **Joe** *walks to the bench. He picks up* **Robert**'s *tankard and drinks.*

I've been good to Molly and you, haven't I?

**Robert**  Aye.

**Joe**  Setting you up with my old cobble. Helpin' yer.

**Robert**  What yer gettin' at, Joe?

**Joe** (*pointing to the cage. Firmly*)  That's an animal. He's no spy. Tomorrow, at the meeting, that's what I'm going to say. Are you goyn to support us, Robert?

**Robert**  'Ow can a? Jus' lately yer've been mekkin' a big fool o'yerself.

**Mary**  They're goyn to hang us, Stockton.

**Stockton** *lets out a loud shriek.*

*A slight pause.*

**Joe** (*putting the tankard on the bench*)  I'd best go t'bed myself. I'll see you in the morning.

**Robert** (*looking at him*)  Aye.

**Joe**  Think about what I've jus' said. I'll expect you to support me. Goodnight.

**Robert**  Goodnight, Joe.

**Joe** *exits towards the town.*
*A moment's pause.*

**Molly** *appears from the house. She walks down towards* **Robert.**

Is Peter tucked up?

**Molly**  He fell straight back t'sleep.

**Molly** *sits down beside* **Robert.** *She cuddles him for a moment, they stop, they gently hold one another. They are still.*

**Mary** *sits down in the cage.*

**Molly** *closes her eyes.* **Robert***'s eyes are open.*
*An owl hoots.*

**Mary**  They're goyn to hang us, Stockton.

**Stockton** *walks on all fours towards* **Mary**. *He sits down beside her.*
**Mary** *strokes him.*

They're goyn to hang us.

**Stockton** *looks at* **Mary**. *He speaks without a trace of an accent.*

**Stockton**  I know.

**Mary** *stops stroking him.*

Do not blame them.

**Mary**  Can' 'elp it, can a. (*Smiling.*) I hoped you would talk.

**Robert** (*without turning round*)  Quiet, boy.

*A moment's pause.* **Robert** *taps out his pipe on the side of the bench. A moment's pause.*

**Mary**  Tekk no notice. Are you really called Stockton?

**Stockton**  No, my real name is Mister Africa. My master, Captain Anderson, bought me from a Zulu warrior. I was his mascot. We travelled the seas together.

**Mary** *strokes* **Stockton** *for a moment. She stops.*

We've carried tea from India, spices from China, coffee from South America and carpets from Persia. It's been a good life.

**Mary** *strokes* **Stockton**.

My master's schooner was pressed into naval service. We were carrying soldiers to London.

**Robert** *closes his eyes.*

**Mary** (*hugging* **Stockton**)  I love you.

**Stockton**  Do not blame these people, Mary.

**Mary**  I'll try not to.

**Stockton**  It isn't their fault. Look at them – what do they know of the world?

**Mary** (*looking at* **Robert** *and* **Molly**)  They've gone t'sleep. (*Stroking him.*)  They're stupid, Stockton.

**Mary** *stops.*

(*Calling to* **Robert** *and* **Molly**) Let me out.

**Robert** *and* **Molly** *are silent.* **Mary** *strokes* **Stockton** *for a moment.*

It's no good shouting, is it?

**Stockton**  No.

**Mary** *stops.*

These people are good people, Mary.

**Mary**  Are they?

**Stockton**  Would you be doing any differently?

**Mary**  A wouldn't be 'angin' meself.

**Stockton**  We'd do exactly the same. We are no better.

**Mary** *strokes* **Stockton.**

**Mary**  A don't want t'die.

**Mary** *stops.*

**Stockton**  In another world, you wouldn't. In this one, you will. We'll leave them our wisdom.

**Mary** (*hugging him*)  I love you.

**Mary** *breaks the hug.*

Don't you mind dyin'?

**Stockton**  Of course.

*The moonlight fades to blackout.*


Scene Three

*The beach at Bay Ness. Two days later. Midday of Thursday July the 13th.*

*An almost empty beach. Sand.*

*The sun is high in the sky. A strong bright light.*

*A gentle sea can still be heard lapping against the shore.*

*At the back of the beach the bodies of* **Mary** *and* **Stockton** *are hanging from two separate hanging posts. At the front, washed up, lies the body of a British soldier dressed in his uniform.*

**Joe** *enters slowly from the direction of Bay Ness. He is wearing his working clothes.*

*The loud bugle-like call of a herring-gull as it flies overhead.*

**Joe** *walks to the British soldier, he turns the body over, he looks at the face.*

**Anne** *enters from the direction of the town. She is wearing her best clothes; shoes, a gown, the red cloak, a bonnet.*

**Joe** *sees* **Anne**.

**Joe** (*surprised*) Mistress?

**Anne** *stops. They are some distance apart.*

**Anne**   A young girl at the town told me where you were.

*A slight pause.*

**Joe**   The bodies are being washed up. Some are ours, from Bay.

*A slight pause.*

I don't recognize this one.

**Anne** *walks to* **Joe**, *she looks at the body.*

**Anne**   It's Stephen Cushion, one of our faggers.

**Joe**   There are bodies the length of the beach. They are English soldiers. How could we not have known?

**Joe** *walks away from* **Anne** *towards the town. He stops.*

The French won't come here.

**Anne**   France is near the southern coast of England.

**Joe**   Is it?

**Anne** *walks a pace or two from the body.*

Did no one at the town stop you?

**Anne**   I walked straight through.

**Joe**   Why've you come?

**Anne**  I came for news of Betsy.

**Joe**  They've gone, disappeared.

**Anne**  Where to, d'you know?

**Joe**  *shakes his head.*

**Joe**  They disappeared yesterday before the hanging.

**Anne** *looks at* **Mary** *and* **Stockton**.

**Anne**  One of them is that boy.

**Joe**  Yes.

**Anne**  I also came for another reason.

*Takes a bundle from beneath her arm. They are her notebooks, they are tied with string.*

I've brought you these. They are my diaries. I don't want them. They're written about Emma.

*A slight pause.*

If you would like them? If not, I'll throw them away. They're too much about the past.

**Joe**  No thank you, Mistress. For the same reason.

**Anne** *puts the diaries back underneath her arm.*
*The bugle-like call of a herring-gull as it flies overhead.*

Has Bay Town changed?

**Anne** (*smiling*)  I tried not to look. I kept my eyes straight ahead. I was frightened.

*A slight pause.*

This school, Joe?

*A slight pause.*

I can promise nothing, but I'd like to help. There's a large old barn in Middlewood. We don't use it. It's half way between Fylingthorpe and Bay Town.

*A slight pause.*

I can read. I can write. I could teach. With you? For all our children? If you would do me that honour.

*A slight pause.*

Don't dither, Joe.

**Joe**  It's such a new idea. I can't believe it would happen.

**Anne**  If we want it to.

*A slight pause.*

**Joe**  Come with me to the town?

**Anne** *hesitates.*

**Anne**  I'm not sure I can face them openly.

**Anne** *walks to* **Joe**. *She looks at the sea.*

I hadn't noticed until now, the men are fishing. (*Looking at* **Joe**.) What will happen?

**Joe**  We'll see, won't we?

**Anne** *and* **Joe** *exit towards the town.*

*The bright sunlight fades to blackout.*

# The Overgrown Path

To Mike and Liz Griffiths

**The Overgrown Path** was first performed at the Royal Court Theatre, London, on 31 May 1985, with the following cast. It was directed by Les Waters and designed by Sue Plummer.

| | |
|---|---|
| **Daniel Howarth** | Peter Vaughan |
| **Mimiko** | Christopher Karallis |
| **Nicholas Marks** | Stuart Wilson |
| **Sarah Jeffs** | Deborah Findlay |
| **Beth Howarth** | Doreen Mantle |
| **Clare** | Martha Parsey |
| **Children** | Saya Akiba, Suzanne Fenelon, Tomoya Hanai, Ayako Kimura, Ken Kotake, Haigi Okada, Sayuri Okada, Nami Sekata |

# *Scenes*

*Act One*

| | |
|---|---|
| Scene One | A school stage |
| Scene Two | The house |
| Scene Three | The house |
| Scene Four | A hillside |

*Act Two*

| | |
|---|---|
| Scene One | A hillside |
| Scene Two | A hillside |
| Scene Three | The beach |
| Scene Four | The beach |

*Apart from Scene One, the play takes place on the Greek island of Tinos, in the Aegean, during the May of 1984.*

# Act One

Scene One

*The small stage of a primary school in modern-day Nagasaki.*

*A black drape hangs at the back. A low wooden bench is set to one side. A long blue ribbon is lying on the wooden floor.*

*A group of nine Japanese* **Children**, *all ten years old, are about to present their play. Eight of the* **Children** *now enter, one after the other, through the drape. The* **Children** *are smartly dressed in their school uniforms.* **One of the Girls** *walks to the front.* **Two of the Boys** *go to either end of the ribbon where they kneel down. The rest of the* **Children** *sit on the bench.*

*The girl at the front, her name is* **Suzuko**, *waits for the* **Children** *to settle, and then she bows to the audience.*

**Suzuko** Mrs Oogushi's class welcome you to their play. (*She narrates the story.*) It is a hot, August morning. The sky has been cloudless for several weeks, and the citizens of Nagasaki grumble as they go about their business.

*The* **Children** *on the bench make the 'sounds' of grumbling.* **One of the Boys** *takes a bird whistle from his pocket and blows it.*

The birds sing. Only the children are happy in this heat.

*The* **Boys**, *kneeling, raise the blue ribbon.*

Imagine the Urakami river on that sultry day in nineteen forty-five. Nature has formed a small pool here. The river flows gently.

*The* **Boys** *flutter the ribbon.*

It was to this pool that five children came, whenever they could sneak away, to play their game called 'find the bell'.

*The five* **Children** *on the bench, three girls and two boys, stand up. As they go to the 'river bank' the narrator continues.*

The game was simple.

*The five* **Children** *mime getting undressed.*

One of the children, Etsuko, had a small gilded bell. When

they were wearing nothing but their pants, Etsuko would throw the bell into the pool.

*The girl playing* **Etsuko** *mimes throwing the bell.*

The children would dive in after it.

*The five children 'dive in'. They look very happy as they swim and dive searching for the bell. The boys with the ribbon, quicken their fluttering.*

It was great fun. Whoever should find the bell first was the winner. But, on this particular morning, the river was cloudy.

*The five* **Children** *'climb out' onto the river bank. One of the boys, his name is* **Koichi**, *speaks first.*

**Koichi**  Etsuko, I can't find it.

**Yasuko**  Nor I.

**Keiko**  Nor I, Etsuko.

**Etsuko** *pulls a long face. The narrator continues.*

**Suzuko**  Etsuko was worried. She had taken the bell from her sister's workbox without her permission. It had to be found. Etsuko well knew the wrath of her angry sister.

**Etsuko** *'dives' into the river. The* **Boys** *flutter the ribbon.*

So, once again, she dived into the Urakami river, and was gone for thirty seconds.

**Etsuko** *disappears beneath the ribbon.*

*A* **Boy** *enters through the drape. He is padded-up to be grotesquely fat, his suit is the colour of metallic black. He is* **'Fat Man'**, *the atomic bomb.*

*The* **Boys** *flutter the ribbon as if there were a violent storm.*

(*Shielding her eyes*)  There was a blinding white flash like lightning, and the next moment Bang! Crack! as thunder rang out. It was Fat Man, the atomic bomb.

*The boy playing* **'Fat Man'** *rushes about. As he touches the* **Children** *playing the divers, they fall over. Then the boy playing* **'Fat Man'** *disappears the way he came, back through the drape.*

*There is silence for a moment before the girl playing* **Etsuko** *appears from beneath the ribbon.*

Etsuko surfaced, having not found the bell, to find everything different. Gone was her primary school. Gone, too, was the College Hospital where, under a protest of screams, Etsuko had been taken by her mother to have her injection. The Mitsubishi Steel Works had disappeared. Etsuko climbed from the river.

**Etsuko** *mimes climbing out.*

Her friends were gone, too. Was this a new game they were playing? Had they found the bell and not told her? If that was so, it wasn't fair. Suddenly it began to snow on Nagasaki.

*The two **Boys** holding the ribbon put it down. They stand up. They have white confetti in their pockets which they throw over **Etsuko**.*

White snowflakes fell over the whole city.

**Etsuko** *hugs herself.*

Etsuko, thinking it was already winter because everything looked so dark and desolate, hugged herself to keep warm. She cried out: 'Mummy'.

**Etsuko** *mimes calling.*

'Mummy, where are you?' But her cry must have been in silence for her mother never appeared.

**Etsuko** *catches a single piece of the confetti.*

And when she touched the snow it didn't melt, but crumbled in her fingers.

*The two **Boys** stop throwing the confetti.*

That is the end of our story, except to say that Etsuko never did find her friends, but grew up and is the name of our teacher, Mrs Oogushi. We hope you liked out play with the happy ending.

*The **Children** stand up. '**Fat Man**' comes through the drape. They hold hands, and bow.*


Scene Two

*The frontage of a house at the village of Panormos on the Greek island of Tinos.*

*The front of the house has two doors. One is the main entrance and leads into the house through the kitchen. the other is to a small, spare bedroom. This door is painted pale blue. The kitchen door is open, coloured strips of plastic hang over the entrance. Beside the entrance is a small, cross-paned kitchen window which is painted the same pale blue. The wall of the house is white-washed, as are the irregular shaped flagstones which pave the ground in front. A small Judas tree, set to the right, is growing out of these flagstones and has cracked and bevelled the areas surrounding it. The base of the tree's thin, twisty trunk has been painted pale blue.*

*An old wooden table stands on the flagstones. Two old bentwood chairs are pushed into it, and there is a third by the kitchen entrance. Elsewhere, there are two larger, heavier, cane wickerwork, easy chairs. One is by the tree, and the other beside the table.*

*The front of the house has a used, lived-in feel to it. The tables and chairs have been bumped and scraped. In odd places the white-wash has weathered and come away. But nothing is decrepit or dirty.*

*Thursday, 10 May. Two o'clock in the afternoon.*

*The sun is high and is powering down. It is very, very hot. A shadow is being cast by the Judas tree across the kitchen entrance.*

*Sitting asleep, on the bentwood chair, in this shadow, is* **Daniel Howarth**. **Daniel** *is so precariously balanced that it looks like he might tumble off the chair at any moment.*

*Above his head is a washing line. It runs from the tree to a hook above the bedroom door. Two squid are hanging on the line, drying in the sun.*

**Daniel** *is seventy-three. He is a big, stocky man with broad shoulders. He has big feet and hands, soft deep-set eyes, and thick dark hair. He is wearing a baggy black suit with a white shirt. He has sandals on his feet.*

*The sound of a bus arriving and coming to a halt, nearby. After a moment its engine stops.*

**Daniel** *snorts in his sleep.*

**Mimiko** *enters. He is carrying a large canvas holdall.*

**Mimiko** *is a Greek boy of sixteen. He is small and thin and wiry. He has jet-black hair and his ears stick out. He is dressed roughly in shoes, trousers, coloured shirt, and jacket. He is over dressed and his clothes are ill-fitting.*

**Mimiko** *hurriedly puts down the holdall and calls back the way he came.*

**Mimiko**  This way. This way.

*After a moment* **Nicholas Marks** *enters.*

**Nicholas** *is thirty-eight. He is tall and distinguished with intelligent eyes. He has an alert, almost boyish face. He is well-dressed in white plimsolls, brown cord trousers, and a check shirt.*

**Nicholas** *stops by his holdall.* **Mimiko** *has walked towards* **Daniel.**

Asleep see. He is an old man. Old men sleep all day, then wake at night. (*Going to wake* **Daniel**.) I wake him for you. It do him good.

**Nicholas**  No, don't.

**Mimiko**  He is an old fool. (*Bending down.*) I tickle his chin.

**Mimiko** *tickles* **Daniel**'s *chin.*

**Nicholas**  I'd rather you left him. I'm happy to wait.

**Daniel** *snorts.*

**Mimiko**  In a moment he shout out his dreams. (*Looking up, his face close to* **Daniel**'s.) Big clown, big nit, daft idiot. Big Koko. (*To* **Nicholas**.) He likes me to be rude. He enjoy a game. (*Taking his hand back.*) I slap him for you now.

**Nicholas**  Don't do that.

**Mimiko** *stands up, he looks dejected.*

Look, thank you for carrying my bag for me.

**Mimiko** (*putting his hand on the top of* **Daniel**'s *head*) This man is famous in England.

**Nicholas**  Yes.

**Mimiko**  You?

**Nicholas**  No. I'm not famous at all in England.

**Mimiko**  You must like our island?

**Nicholas**  What I've seen of it so far, very much.

**Mimiko** (*going to him*) I like England. We are friends.

*He offers his hand.* **Nicholas** *shakes it.*

For carrying your case I receive money. Daniel would give me, but he is asleep.

**Nicholas** (*delving into his pocket*)  Yes, of course.

**Mimiko**  I cannot take coin. I have my pride.

**Nicholas** *puts the coins back. He takes his leather wallet from his back pocket.*

Are you always mean when it comes to money?

**Nicholas**  I'm sorry?

**Mimiko**  I not take anything now. You have hurt me. We are not friends. Goodbye.

**Mimiko** *goes off looking deliberately forlorn.*
**Nicholas**, *a note in his hand, looks perplexed.*

*A slight pause.*

**Daniel** *snorts.*
**Nicholas** *looks at* **Daniel** *for a moment. He walks to the edge of the flagstones and looks at the view. He puts the note in the wallet and the wallet back in his pocket.*

*A bird, a bee-eater, calls nearby.*
**Daniel** *gives a loud snort.*
**Nicholas** *looks at him.*
**Daniel** *wakes as if he had never been asleep.*

**Daniel**  Ah, you've arrived. (*Getting up, going to him.*) Daniel Howarth. You've come to ask about my work on the hydrogen bomb.

**Nicholas**  I'm sorry if I woke you.

**Daniel**  No, no, I wasn't asleep, just dozing. You must be Richard. Nice of you to come.

**Nicholas** (*shaking his hand*)  Nicholas, not Richard. Nicholas Marks.

**Daniel**  Let's not get ourselves confused.

*Their hands part.*

Nicholas. Now then, you'd like a drink.

*He goes through the plastic strips into the kitchen.*

**Nicholas** *walks to the edge of the flagstones, he looks down over the village once again.*

*A slight pause.*
*The bee-eater calls.*
*A slight pause.*

**Daniel** *returns, he is carrying a tray. On it are two glasses of water; two smaller, empty glasses; and a bottle of ouzo.*

(*Going to the table*) Why did I think you were a Richard.

*He puts the tray down.*

**Nicholas** You live in a beautiful part of the world, Professor Howarth.

**Daniel** (*picking up the bottle of ouzo*) D'you drink this stuff?

**Nicholas** Thank you very much.

**Daniel** (*taking the top off*) It's aniseedy. The British, I believe, feed aniseed to cattle.

*He pours ouzo into the two small glasses.*

**Nicholas** I think that's silage

**Daniel** The two are not the same. (*Screwing the top back.*) We shouldn't take too much notice of it – the British will feed anything to anything.

**Nicholas** I spent part of my childhood on a farm.

**Daniel** Really? Tell me what you like and we'll get it in. Shyness will make your stay miserable.

*He picks up the glasses of ouzo.*

There is water on the table.

**Nicholas** (*taking his glass from* **Daniel**) Thank you.

*They walk to the edge of the flagstones.*

**Daniel** Good journey?

**Nicholas** Not too bad.

**Daniel** The Greeks are terribly unreliable.

*They sip their drinks.*

**Nicholas** I was thinking how beautiful the island is.

**Daniel**  Have you been to Greece before, Nicholas?

**Nicholas**  No.

**Daniel**  Most things have a beauty. The truth comes with time.

**Nicholas**  (*after a moment's pause*)  I noticed so many small churches on the way.

**Daniel**  There are a few. (*After a moment's pause.*) No, Tinos is a Greek island, if that makes sense to you. We get very few European tourists. The town of Tinos has a shrine. A holy icon of the Virgin Mary was found in eighteen twenty-three, by St Pelagia. The islands became a place of pilgrimage for the Greeks, like Lourdes for the French. The island is sacred. It holds miracles. Has magic.

**Nicholas**  Is that why you chose it?

**Daniel**  (*smiling*)  I wonder, do you?

**Nicholas**  (*shrugging*)  I don't know.

**Daniel**  It has a peace which we like. Especially here, away from the main town. The English are arrogant abroad – don't you find?

**Nicholas**  Sometimes, yes.

**Daniel**  I expect it's because we're arrogant at home. We have tiny minds. I say that with regret.

**Nicholas**  When did you first come here?

**Daniel**  Now you ask a question. Would it be nineteen seventy-five? (*Incredulously*) I believe it was, you know.

**Nicholas**  (*smiling*)  You obviously like it.

**Daniel**  Oh, I think so, don't you?

**Nicholas**  Yes.

**Daniel**  I see no reason to move.

**Daniel** *indicates the chairs at the table.*

Let me say from the outset that we can't put you up. (*Walking to a bentwood chair.*) Much as we'd like to. Unfortunately my daughter is staying with us.

**Nicholas** (*following him*) I didn't expect you to.

**Daniel** (*sitting down*) How odd. I thought we'd put in a letter that we would.

**Nicholas** (*sitting in the other bentwood chair*) You did, but it doesn't matter.

**Daniel** You're being kind. It's of no consequence, she's here and that's that. I've arranged a room for you.

**Nicholas** Thank you.

**Daniel** There's no hotel. She's a widow – you'll be having her son's room. I've left the financial arrangements up to you. She won't charge you much – they're very generous. She'll allow you your privacy, that's the main thing, isn't it? I'll take you to her, later.

**Nicholas** I hope I'm not putting her son out?

**Daniel** No, no, she's used to guests. You'll find she doesn't speak English.

**Nicholas** My Greek isn't very good. (*Smiling.*) We'll manage.

**Daniel** Tonight you'll eat with us. After that, it's entirely up to you. There are two tavernas in the village. Both are nice. You are welcome here whenever you feel like it.

**Nicholas** Thank you.

**Daniel** *sits back, his glass of ouzo in his hand. He is drinking very little.*

**Daniel** You work in a sweet shop, Nicholas?

**Nicholas** Yes.

**Daniel** I found that interesting.

**Nicholas** I don't know that it is really.

**Daniel** (*an excitement in his voice*) Why, tell me why that is?

**Nicholas** (*after thinking for a moment*) It's routine, for the most part. The hours are long if you open as we do.

**Daniel** And you were brought up on a farm?

**Nicholas** I used to go to the farm for my holidays.

**Daniel** I see.

**Nicholas** (*smiling*) I know the shop like my hand.

**Daniel** How fascinating.

**Nicholas** It's in Yorkshire – Cleveland.

**Daniel** D'you sell pineapple chunks?

**Nicholas** Yes. And cigarettes. And kiddies' toys. Birthday and anniversary cards. Daily Papers. You can imagine the sort of shop.

**Daniel** (*nodding*) Mmm.

**Nicholas** I have a manageress – Mrs Robson – which is why I'm able to get away.

**Daniel** (*pondering*) Mmm.

**Nicholas** There's a similar shop in every high street.

**Daniel** (*nodding*) Mmm.

**Nicholas** (*after a moment's pause*) It's good of you to see me, Professor Howarth.

**Daniel** Is it? I'm not sure that it is.

**Nicholas** I was told you don't see many people.

**Daniel** (*chortling slightly*) I believe, not many people want to see me. It flatters my ego if they do.

**Daniel** *stretches forward and picks up the bottle of ouzo, he unscrews the top. He offers some to* **Nicholas**.

**Nicholas** A little, please.

*He pours some into* **Nicholas**'s *glass*.

Thank you, that's plenty.

**Daniel** *doesn't have any himself.*

**Daniel** (*putting the bottle down*) I'll show you the island whilst you're here. We might enjoy that together. The miracles I mean.

**Nicholas** I hope I won't intrude on your privacy.

**Daniel** No, no.

**Daniel** *takes a packet of plain Senior Service cigarettes from his jacket pocket. He lights one with a match.*

(*Putting the cigarettes and matches away*)  Tell me, Richard, d'you like stories?

**Nicholas**  Nicholas.

**Daniel**  Nicholas. I love stories. They have in them the richness of our lives.

**Daniel** *stands up.*

**Nicholas**  I don't know quite what you mean? Please explain.

**Daniel** (*the cigarette in his mouth, taking off his jacket*)  I suppose I mean myths. Legends. Parables.

**Nicholas**  I read all sorts of stories as a kid. Fairy-tales.

**Daniel**  I did too.

**Daniel** *puts the jacket over the bentwood chair. His shirt sleeves are rolled up; he is wearing two watches, one on each wrist. He takes the cigarette from his mouth.*

(*Walking to the tree*)  You're young still. I don't expect stories are important to you yet.

**Nicholas**  D'you mean stories help to explain our lives?

**Daniel** *sits on the cane chair in the shade of the tree.*

**Daniel**  It may be an age thing. Are you married?

**Nicholas**  No. No, I'm not.

**Daniel**  If Beth should fuss you, ignore her. Women are like that.

**Nicholas**  Beth is your wife.

**Daniel** (*drawing on his cigarette*)  My second wife. What were we talking about, Richard?

**Nicholas** (*half smiling*)  I think you get my name wrong on purpose.

**Daniel** (*chortling slightly*)  Do I? Do I? It's Nicholas, isn't it? (*Leaning forward.*) I may tell you stories because I hate facts. The world today is far too factual, don't you find? The pleasure of a story is in its interpretation. It has a philosophy. A fact has nothing. Like a name. (*Sitting back.*) I may call you Richard, if that's all right?

*He puffs on his cigarette.*

*A slight pause.*

**Nicholas** *stands up with his glass of ouzo, he walks to the edge of the flagstones and looks at the view.*

I'm sorry I didn't meet you off the bus. I had meant to.

**Nicholas** (*turning to him*) I haven't really any specific questions.

**Daniel** Good.

**Nicholas** I was worried you'd think that was lazy.

**Daniel** No, no.

**Nicholas** It might take me a few days to get my bearings.

**Daniel** I'm sure.

*A slight pause.*

**Nicholas** (*tentatively*) And not having done anything academic for so long – well, that's my problem, not yours.

**Daniel** No, no.

**Nicholas** (*slightly tentatively*) I want you to know that I'm not here to make judgements.

**Daniel** (*after a moment's pause*) We liked your letters. We found them honest.

**Nicholas** (*suddenly with shyness*) Thank you.

*A slight pause.*

I think I told you I'd had enough of the shop.

*Cigarette ash falls onto* **Daniel**'s *trousers. He brushes it off. He uses the ashtray which is beside him on the flagstones.*

**Daniel** I don't know why, but never mind. Beth and I found it so intriguing.

**Nicholas** (*smiling*) People do.

*A slight pause.*

When did you marry Beth, Professor Howarth?

**Daniel** (*brightly*) Would it be nineteen sixty-two? I believe it was, you know. The grass was full of white snowdrops.

*A bus horn honks several times, nearby.*

You worked in London?

**Nicholas** Yes, for a while, after university.

**Daniel** Beth has your letters. (*After drawing on his cigarette.*) We were married in a London February. What a mantle of depression London had then – didn't you find?

**Nicholas** Sometimes.

**Daniel** It has one colour – that of meanness. I learnt to loathe the bloody place.

**Nicholas** *smiles.*

I tried not to be there as much as I could.

*The bus horn honks again.*

(*Standing up*) There's your bus about to go back.

**Nicholas** Am I disturbing you?

**Daniel** (*joining* **Nicholas** *at the edge of the flagstones*) No, No.

**Nicholas** Perhaps for our talks we should arrange a timetable?

**Daniel** As you wish.

**Sarah Jeffs** *enters, running. She is carrying a small, brightly coloured beach bag.*

**Sarah** *is thirty-six. She is small and thin with a boyish frame and face. Her blonde hair is short. She is wearing a pair of off-white long shorts, a red teeshirt and flip-flops.*

**Sarah** (*dashing to the spare bedroom door*) I want to catch the bus before he goes.

*She opens the door and hurries in.*

**Daniel** (*calling after her*) There's no bus back, pet. Not today. You'll be stuck in Tinos.

**Sarah** (*from inside*) No, I know. (*Reappearing without her bag. Carrying an envelope.*) I want him to post a letter for me.

**Daniel** This is Nicholas, pet.

**Sarah** Hello.

**Nicholas** Hello.

**Sarah** I'll see you later.

**Sarah** *dashes off.*

*The bus engine turns over. After a few rickety attempts, it starts.*
**Nicholas** *and* **Daniel** *watch.*

**Nicholas**   How often is the bus?

**Daniel**   There's two a day – one in the morning, one in the afternoon. They drive like bloody madmen.

**Nicholas** *smiles.*

That's Yanni. They think they're like cats with nine lives. (*Turning, walking to the tree.*) Yanni's used three of his while I've been on the bus.

**Daniel** *stands above the ashtray. He flicks his cigarette, ash swirls down towards it. He looks at* **Nicholas.**

You're from Skelton – is that right?

**Nicholas**   Yes.

**Daniel**   Tell me about it?

**Nicholas**   It's a small market town in the Cleveland Hills, in what was once Yorkshire.

**Daniel**   I'm Lancashire, of course. (*Chortling slightly.*) We're sworn enemies. Manchester – where it rains. Soddin' awful place. (*Chortling.*) I think I'd kick the bucket if I had to go there now.

**Nicholas** (*slightly tentatively*)   I went and looked for your house.

**Daniel**   Did you indeed? That was thorough.

**Nicholas**   It's – er – not there.

**Daniel**   I know. (*Puffing on his cigarette.*) It was pulled down with my mother inside it. The old fool wouldn't budge. (*Bending down.*) She was one of those.

*The bus horn honks. The bus pulls away into the distance.*
**Daniel** *stubs out his cigarette.*

**Nicholas**   I met your old science teacher.

**Daniel** (*straightening up*)   Good God. (*With feeling.*) Is he still alive? (*Thinking.*) Wait a minute, wait a minute – I used to go and visit him.

**Nicholas**  Mr Cuthbertson.

**Daniel** (*smiling*)  That's it.

**Nicholas**  He's ninety-six. He asked me to give you his regards.

**Daniel** (*almost speechless*)  How wonderful.

*A slight pause.*

(*A grunt of pleasure*)  Arr. How did you find him?

**Nicholas**  I went to the school.

**Daniel** (*stumbling with pleasure*)  He, he, he, like all good teachers, made you think you were learning something for the first time – that your knowledge was unique. Then he broadened the context, and showed you the avenues. (*Smiling.*) That's made my day. Fancy him still being alive. After all these years.

**Nicholas** *smiles.*

**Nicholas**  He told me you were a scholarship boy?

**Daniel**  Oh, I expect I was. (*A glazed look behind his eyes.*) Manchester Grammar School. Mr Cuthbertson. Thank you, Nicholas.

**Nicholas**  He remembers giving your mother some money to buy you shoes.

**Daniel**  There's nothing in class, you know. I'm aware your generation thinks there is.

**Nicholas**  It was a well-heeled school.

**Daniel**  Still is, I believe.

**Nicholas**  How much of an outsider did you feel?

**Daniel**  Good God. Not a bit. I had a mind, I used it.

**Mimiko** *enters. He has his hands in his pockets, he is sulking.*

Ah, Mimiko.

**Mimiko** *goes to* **Daniel**.

I want you to meet an English friend of mine.

**Daniel** *turns* **Mimiko** *round to face* **Nicholas**, *he puts his hands on his shoulders.*

This is Nicholas.

**Mimiko** *sticks his tongue out.*

You'll be seeing a lot of Mimiko.

**Nicholas** (*brightly*) Hello.

**Mimiko** This man is rubbish. I carry his case. He is the rudest man in Greece.

**Daniel** Oh dear.

**Mimiko** *walks from* **Daniel**'s *hands. He goes to* **Daniel**'s *jacket on the bentwood chair.*

Mimiko is easily upset. Aren't you, Mimiko?

**Mimiko** *has found the cigarettes and matches in* **Daniel**'s *jacket.*

**Mimiko** Daniel, a cigarette? (*Taking one from the packet.*) Beth she go off, early this morning, where she go to?

**Daniel** Pyrgos.

**Mimiko** Who for?

**Mimiko** *lights the cigarette.*

**Daniel** (*sitting down in the cane chair*) There is an outbreak of measles in the village, amongst the children.

**Mimiko** (*putting the cigarettes and matches back in the pocket*) The spots have come again. (*To* **Nicholas**.) You are a friend of Beth too?

**Nicholas** No. This is my first visit.

**Mimiko** (*sitting in the bentwood chair*) Who he stay with?

**Daniel** Mrs Melianos.

**Mimiko** She is a good woman. She look after you. (*Turning to* **Daniel**.) This morning I see a funny thing. A white bird. The pink eyes of a God. He is flying along. I think he is a sparrow. Another bird, a bigger bird, I think a jackdaw, swoop from the sky and attack him.

**Daniel** The sparrow was an albino.

**Mimiko** This I know. (*Miming with his hand.*) The bigger bird chase him like a race.

**Nicholas** *sips his ouzo.*

**Daniel** Did the jackdaw kill the sparrow?

**Mimiko** This I did not see. From the way it was going, I think so. (*To* **Nicholas**.) These birds attack what they do not understand. (*To* **Daniel**.) They cause a nuisance in the sky.

**Daniel** *smiles.*

(*To* **Nicholas**) In return for cigarettes, I explain to Daniel.

**Daniel** Whenever Mimiko wants a cigarette, he has a story to tell.

**Mimiko** I smoke too much. It is the way I get a fag. You smoke, Nicholas?

**Nicholas** No, I used to. I gave it up.

*He walks towards the other bentwood chair.*

**Mimiko** (*incredulous*) You have no stories now?

**Nicholas** *sits.*

Some days we smoke like a big chimney. At the end of the day we are demolished like an old chimney. We have told a hundred stories.

**Daniel** *smiles.*

(*Pushing it under* **Nicholas**'s *nose*) This is an English cigarette.

**Nicholas** *moves his head.*

Senior Service. The best. Daniel only puff English.

**Daniel** Sarah sends, or brings me them.

**Mimiko** It is the only thing about England Daniel miss. Senior Service.

**Daniel** *chortles.*

I make him laugh the old fool. Greek cigarettes are mud to him. I think it is rude. But we ignore it. He is like a Greek when he tries. (*To* **Daniel**.) Nicholas is a new friend?

**Daniel** Yes.

**Mimiko** Ah, I see. You do not know Sarah?

**Nicholas** No.

**Mimiko**  Sarah, she is special. His daughter. Or Beth?

**Nicholas**  No.

**Mimiko**  Beth, she is an American, she is not like Daniel.

**Daniel**  That's enough, Mimiko.

**Mimiko**  Beth, she is a doctor. I have watched her, she is a clever woman. The spots they go like a magic trick.

**Daniel**  Enough.

**Mimiko**  He likes it when I am rude. He is a clown. (*To* **Daniel**.) Big Koko.

**Daniel**  That's your name. You're the clown.

**Mimiko**  He give us all names. What name he give you?

**Nicholas**  Er – Richard.

**Mimiko** (*twisting his finger away from the side of his head*)  It is so his mind can wander in a fantasy about us.

**Daniel**  Thank you, Mimiko.

**Mimiko** (*turning to* **Daniel**)  You tell me this many times. (*To* **Nicholas**.) He like to make things up.

**Sarah** *enters. She is carrying another envelope.*

What name he give you, Sarah?

**Sarah**  I don't think he dare.

**Daniel**  Did you catch Yanni, pet?

**Sarah**  Yes. There's a letter for Beth.

**Daniel**  Where from?

**Sarah**  Athens. (*Putting the envelope on the table*.) From the hospital.

**Sarah** *sits on the table, her legs dangling.*

Aren't you hot?

**Mimiko**  The heat is nothing.

**Sarah**  I don't know how you do it.

**Mimiko**  I think of winter.

**Daniel**  You didn't notice her in the village?

**Sarah**  No. Where did she go this morning?

**Daniel** (*standing up*) Pyrgos.

**Mimiko**  The spots are back.

**Daniel** (*walking to the edge of the flagstones*) One of the teenagers came down. She's usually back before now. (*Searching with his eyes.*) I wish she wouldn't take so much on. (*Turning to her.*) Have a word with her, will you? She listens to you.

**Sarah** (*jumping off the table, going to him*) Don't be silly. I'm sure she's fine.

**Sarah** *kisses* **Daniel** *on the forehead.*

**Daniel** (*smiling*) This evening. Tell her off for me. Shout at her and things. Make a fuss.

**Sarah** (*taking his arm*) Come on, come for a swim.

**Daniel**  No. You go.

**Mimiko**  I race you, Sarah. *Bame. Dtrechomme.*

**Sarah**  What does that mean?

**Mimiko** (*getting up, running off*) Go. Run.

**Mimiko** *goes.*

**Sarah**  Come on.

**Daniel**  You go, love.

**Sarah** *hesitates.*

If he beats you, we'll never hear the last of it.

**Sarah** *dashes into the spare bedroom. She returns a second later with her beach bag.*

**Sarah** (*to* **Nicholas**) You coming?

**Nicholas**  I'll stay here, thanks.

**Sarah** *goes.*

**Daniel**  If you would like some more, help yourself.

**Nicholas** *pours a drop of ouzo into his empty glass.*

We're none of us great drinkers now, but don't let it stop you.

**Nicholas** *stands up. He joins* **Daniel** *at the flagstones.*

I hope you won't take Mimiko too seriously.

**Nicholas**  His knowledge of English is remarkable.

**Daniel**  Yes, it is.

*The bee-eater calls.*

(*Smiling*)  The little bugger knows he can be charming.

**Nicholas**  How old is he?

**Daniel**  Sixteen.

**Nicholas** *pulls a face.*

*The bee-eater calls.*

**Daniel** *looks as if he is about to say something.*

(*Changing his mind*)  No, no, you're not married, are you.

**Daniel** *walks to the cane chair. For the moment he seems in a world of his own. He sits down.*

**Nicholas**  Maybe I should go and find my room?

**Daniel**  We'll give her a few more minutes, let Siesta be over.

*A slight pause.*

Forgive my pacing about. I will find time to relax with you. (*After a moment's pause.*) It's so bloody hot today.

*A slight pause.*

**Daniel** *chortles.*

Mr Cuthbertson. Well I wonder what he's doing now? D'you play that game?

**Nicholas** *looks perplexed.*

No, no, it's nothing, you'll think me daft.

**Nicholas**  Which game is that?

*The bee-eater calls.*

**Daniel**  Oh, it's just a silly thing Mimiko and I play – he leads me on in his inimitable way. We think of someone, and we imagine what they might be doing at the moment we're talking about them. We have the fantasy game. The realistic game.

Sometimes we imagine characters from another century. I need little encouragement, Nicholas.

**Nicholas** *smiles.*

It's fantastic fun with people you don't much like. So watch it. (*Chortling.*) We put them on the lavatory. Or in other despicable situations.

**Beth Howarth** *enters. She is pushing an old, black bicycle. Her doctor's bag is on the back.*

**Beth** *is sixty-nine. She is a strong-looking woman with a homely, gentle face. Her greying hair is tied in a bun. She has greater cares than her appearance and is wearing a flowered, short-sleeved, cotton dress. She has sandals on her feet. Her voice is soft and has barely a trace of an American accent.*

**Beth** *is tired, and has been for several months, but you would hardly know it. She wheels her bicycle towards the spare bedroom door.*

**Beth** What on earth are you two talking about?

**Daniel** (*standing up*) Here you are. Beth, this is Nicholas.

**Beth** (*resting her bicycle against the wall*) I can see that. (*Smiling.*) Hello. You managed to find us.

**Nicholas** Yes, thank you.

**Beth** Hopefully Daniel's not been bullying you too much?

**Nicholas** Not at all, Dr Howarth. Quite the opposite.

**Beth** *has the bicycle settled. She looks at* **Nicholas**.

**Beth** He is the most terrible tyrant. (*Offering her hand.*) We've been waiting to meet you.

**Nicholas** And you.

*They shake hands.*

**Daniel** Was it measles?

**Beth** Yes, that's why I've been so long. (*Breathing deeply.*) One little girl – (*To* **Daniel**.) Soula, remember her? – has got it quite badly, that's why I've been so long.

**Daniel** *is walking to the bicycle.*

Her temperature's way, way up.

**Beth** *leans against the table.*

**Daniel** (*at the bicycle*) D'you want your bag, love?

**Beth** Yes, please.

**Daniel** *unclips the bag from the back of the bicycle.*

**Daniel** (*taking it to the table*) Have you cycled from Pyrgos?

**Beth** (*still catching her breath*) It's downhill most of the way. There's just that bit in the middle.

**Daniel** *puts the bag on the table.*

**Daniel** (*going back to the bike*) Sarah's going to tell you off this evening.

**Daniel** *wheels the bicycle into the spare bedroom.*

**Beth** (*her breathing getting easier*) Has Daniel explained that their own doctor is away?

**Nicholas** No.

**Beth** I help out. It can be a slog.

**Daniel** (*from inside*) There's a letter for you.

**Beth** (*calling back*) I noticed. I sent a blood sample for analysis.

**Daniel** *comes out.*

Does Sarah mind the bike in there?

**Daniel** I shouldn't think so.

**Beth** Have you asked her?

**Daniel** Should I have done? She'd have said, wouldn't she?

**Beth** It's not very comfortable, sleeping with a bike. Have you explained to Nicholas?

**Daniel** (*standing beside her*) Stop interfering, woman.

**Beth** It could go in the kitchen.

**Daniel** Not on your nelly. I'd be tripping over it every other second.

**Beth** I saw Mrs Melianos. She's up.

**Daniel** Oh, right.

**Beth** She was asking. (*Smiling at him.*) I wasn't sure if Nicholas had made it.

**Daniel** He was brought up on a farm.

**Beth** Oh, were you?

**Nicholas** Er – no.

*The bee-eater calls.*

It was my aunt and uncle's farm. I spent my summers there.

**Daniel** He's an expert on silage.

**Nicholas** (*shaking his head slightly*) No. I'm not.

**Beth** Stop it, you old goat.

**Daniel** Did they keep pigs?

**Daniel** *chortles, boyishly.*

**Beth** (*more quietly*) Daniel.

**Daniel** (*perching beside* **Beth** *on the table*) No, I used to love pigs. I could watch them for hours. Didn't we?

**Beth** *takes* **Daniel**'s *hand.*

(*To* **Nicholas**) In the fields between Cambridge and Bedford. In those corrugated huts. When they first arrived they stopped the traffic. (*Looking at* **Beth**.) We'd have liked to have been farmers.

**Beth** (*gently squeezing* **Daniel**'s *hand*) Why don't you take Nicholas up.

**Daniel** (*smiling*) We went round one, didn't we? (*To* **Nicholas**.) It was like a small factory. D'you know, he bred over six thousand pigs a year. Milled his own wheat. Added the fishmeal. Cubed it into pellets with molasses. And dropped the pellets into the field in a hopper behind the tractor. (*To* **Beth**.) We stayed in Cambridge because of those pigs.

**Beth** Take him up. Don't keep her waiting.

**Daniel** (*going to his jacket*) I loathed Cambridge. (*Taking his jacket off the chair.*) Hated academics.

**Beth** Daniel exaggerates.

**Daniel** (*putting his jacket on*) Beth likes to keep things smooth.

**Nicholas** *smiles.*

Farms are for growing up on. I envy you.

**Nicholas**  Which way do we go?

**Daniel** (*walking to* **Nicholas**'s *holdall*)  It's just up the hill a little. Nicholas was asking when we were married, I couldn't remember.

**Beth**  Nineteen sixty-two.

**Daniel** (*picking up the holdall*)  Oh, I did remember. I said something with a two in it.

**Nicholas**  I'll take that.

**Daniel**  No, no.

**Daniel** *walks off with the holdall.*

**Nicholas**  I'll see you later. Thank you, Dr Howarth.

**Beth** (*smiling*)  It's a pleasure.

**Nicholas** *goes, following* **Daniel**. **Beth** *watches them go.*

*A slight pause.*

*The bee-eater calls.*

**Beth** *picks up the letter, opens it, and starts to read.*
*The bright sunlight fades to blackout.*


Scene Three

*The house.*
*Early the following morning. Friday, 11 May. Five o'clock.*

*There is a clear, starlit sky which can be seen above the house. A bright, semicircular moon is shining amongst them.*

*The squid have gone from the washing line.*
*The sound of insects.*

**Beth** *is standing, alone. Her hair, now hanging in a long plait, is dishevelled from sleep. She is wearing a white nightdress. She has the letter in her hand, she is reading.*

*A pause.*

**Daniel** *enters through the open kitchen door. He is wearing striped pyjamas – the sort that tie at the waist with a cord.*

*He goes to her. They embrace.* **Daniel** *kisses her and then pulls back slightly. He looks into her eyes.*

**Daniel** Won't you tell me?

**Beth** Tell you what, you old goat.

**Daniel** Oh I don't know – anything, something – as long as it's the truth.

**Beth** *puts the letter in the envelope.*

It's no good putting that away, I'm going to read it.

**Beth** *puts the letter behind her back.*

I shall count to four.

*He doesn't.*
*A slight pause.*

**Beth** I sent a blood sample to Athens. Mine, my blood.

**Daniel** And?

**Beth** It was positive. (*Taking his hand.*) I've not been well, Daniel, you know that.

**Daniel** (*gently*) Hiding like a bloody cowering mouse.

**Beth** That isn't quite fair.

**Daniel** (*impassioned*) Why, Beth?

**Beth** (*after a moment's pause*) Because it's serious. I wanted to be certain.

**Daniel** Aren't we here to share f'God's sake?

**Beth** It's leukaemia.

**Daniel** (*looking down*) Oh, fuck.

**Beth** (*tightly holding his hand*) Quite acute, I guess. But not desperate yet.

**Daniel** Shit. (*Looking back up.*) How advanced? How long?

**Beth** Four or five months, perhaps six maybe. Maybe even a year. Two. It has been known, Daniel.

**Daniel** (*squeezing her hand*) Oh, Beth.

*A pause.*

*They embrace*
*Tears come into* **Beth***'s eyes.*

**Beth** I'm not unhappy about it. Don't you be, love. I love you.

*A pause.*

**Daniel** What's the treatment, pet.

**Beth** (*shaking her head slightly*) I don't want it.

*They pull back from the embrace.*

It's chemotherapy. It's dreadful, it's worse than the disease. I've seen patients go through it.

**Daniel** (*wiping* **Beth***'s tears away with his thumb*) You're crying.

*A slight pause.*

(*Taking both her hands*) I love you too, you know.

**Beth** (*smiling*) What a pair of silly donkeys we are.

**Daniel** (*flapping her arms. Brightly*) Why?

**Beth** When I was a girl I longed to love a man forever. Now I've my chance. Do you forgive me?

**Daniel** Oh, Beth.

**Beth** For not telling you before?

**Daniel** (*putting his hands on her waist*) When did it start?

**Beth** I first noticed it before Christmas, I guess. I kept feeling tired, really tired.

**Daniel** I know.

**Beth** Then an ulcer arrived in my mouth. And my throat was sore – really like sandpaper.

**Daniel** I don't think I will forgive you, you know.

**Beth** If I hadn't been a doctor, I'd have told you. I knew what it was from the start – somehow. I saw the the symptoms too often in Japan. The anaemia, the breathlessness.

**Daniel** Yes.

*A slight pause.*

**Beth**  I want to go back.

**Daniel** *looks at her.*

To Japan.

**Daniel**  We'll go.

**Beth**  I'd like to try and find Etsuko. I'd really like to know if she's alive or dead.

**Daniel**  Yes.

**Beth** (*brightly*)  I've kept wondering if I was just being silly.

**Daniel**  She may be dead, you know that?

**Beth** (*smiling*)  I know.

**Daniel** (*smiling*)  You always said you wanted to think of her as being alive.

**Beth**  I guess I have to know for sure.

*They are looking into each other's eyes. They kiss.*

*A shooting-star chases across the sky behind them.*

*They pull back from the embrace.*

What time is it?

**Daniel**  Five o'clock, half-past five.

**Beth** *smiles.*

*They hold hands.*

Who's going to tell Sarah?

**Beth**  Can't we leave it for a while. I don't want a fuss, Daniel.

**Daniel**  That's not very fair on her.

**Beth**  Let me decide. (*Looking at him.*) Please.

**Daniel**  Of course, love. I don't want you to do anything you don't want.

**Beth** (*smiling*)  And no secret words – promise?

**Daniel** (*jokingly humming and hawing*)  Mm-mm-mm-mm-mm-mm. Promise.

**Beth**  You old goat.

**Daniel** *smiles. He starts to chortle.*

What're you laughing at?

**Daniel** (*he has stopped*) I shouldn't be. Nicholas. He's come all this way. We're not going to be here.

**Beth**  I liked him.

**Daniel** (*half-surprised*) Did you?

**Beth**  Yes, I thought he was very genuine.

*The very first faint sunlight of dawn can be seen.*

**Daniel**  No, I liked him too. He's none of the aggression of an academic. It's what you thought.

**Beth**  Does he want to go back to Cambridge?

**Daniel**  I presume so. (*Smiling.*) He's odd. He's just like a sweet shop, don't you think?

**Beth**  What's a sweet shop?

**Daniel**  He is.

**Beth** (*smiling*) Don't be obtuse. Don't play him a dance, will you?

**Daniel**  Why, have I done? Am I such an old cunt?

**Beth**  He's shy.

**Daniel**  I know. And pompous, like all would-be academics. You see, I bet.

**Beth** *puts her hand to the side of her face.*

What's the matter?

**Beth**  That ulcer. I've still got it, I can't shift it. (*Hiding her pain.*) It's right on the inside of the gum.

**Daniel** (*heartfelt*) Oh, Beth.

**Beth** (*brightly*) Don't you worry.

**Daniel** *takes both her hands.* **Beth** *smiles.*

**Daniel**  It's at times like this I feel so selfish.

*A single tear rolls down* **Daniel**'s *cheek.* **Beth** *frees one of her hands* *and wipes it away with her fingers.*

**Beth** No tears, my Love.

**Daniel**'s *eyes flood with tears.*

**Daniel** I used to dream of feeling like this. Like crying. (*Sobbing.*) Oh, Beth.

**Beth** *takes him in her arms.*

**Beth** It's all right, love, it's all right.

**Daniel** (*still sobbing*) For years I had no feelings.

**Beth** You did. It just feels that way now. No one is all wrong in what they do.

**Daniel** I do so love you.

*He is still sobbing.*

**Beth** Ssh. Ssh.

**Daniel** I still have the feeling I could have stopped work. At least helped a little when I had.

**Beth** You did, love, you did.

**Daniel** That's my arrogance, I expect.

*A slight pause.*

I'm not sure I can face Etsuko.

**Beth** (*gently*) I know, I know. (*After a moment's pause.*) You will.

*A slight pause.*

We both need to, Daniel.

**Daniel** Why didn't we go years and years ago?

**Beth** Because I was afraid.

*A slight pause.*

**Daniel** (*pulling back slightly from the embrace*) How odd we all are. How little we understand of ourselves. But we stumble on, refusing to be pricked by anything.

*A slight pause.*

That is why I like Greece, you know – they've been pricked and pricked and pricked.

*A cockerel crows, nearby.*

*The dawn sunlight is still coming up. The stars have almost gone.*

**Daniel** *has stopped sobbing. They break the embrace.*

It's getting light.

**Daniel** *has a few remaining tears,* **Beth** *brushes them away with her thumb. She still has the letter.*

You didn't let me read the letter.

**Beth** *takes her thumb away.*

I will try and change.

**Beth** (*smiling*) Don't be an old goat.

*The dawn light fades to blackout.*


Scene Four

*A hillside overlooking the town of Panormos and its small harbour.*

*The ground rises in a steady, even incline from the bottom to the top. At the top of the hill are two lemon trees. Standing in between them is a beehive. The beehive is brightly painted in horizontal lines (using up paint) in blue, yellow, orange, red and green. The ground is hard and baked. What grass there is is scorched and brown.*

*Four days later. Tuesday, 15 May. Three o'clock in the afternoon.*

*The sun, at its highest point in the sky, is burning down. The hillside is bathed in sunlight.*

**Sarah** *is lying at the bottom of the hill reading a hardback copy of an Evelyn Waugh novel. Her bag is beside her. She is wearing her long shorts and a yellow teeshirt. Her shoes are on the grass.*

**Nicholas** *appears at the top of the slope beside one of the lemon trees. He is wearing jeans, a white teeshirt, and plimsolls.*

*He walks down towards her.* **Sarah** *looks up.*

**Nicholas** Your father brought me here on Saturday. He said it was one of your favourite places.

*He stops near her.*

How long d'you think they'll be gone?

**Sarah**  Five years, four years, three years.

**Nicholas**  He said he thought a week. I was wondering whether to stay or not?

**Sarah** *reads her book.* **Nicholas** *sits down.*

It's bloody inconvenient.

**Sarah**  Have you got a worm in your mouth?

**Nicholas**  What?

**Sarah**  Nothing.

**Nicholas**  What?

**Sarah**  It sounds like there's something wriggling about.

**Nicholas**  D'you mind talking about him, Sarah?

**Sarah**  Yes, I do mind.

*She reads her book.*

Have a holiday.

**Nicholas**  What was he like as a father?

**Sarah**  Are you sure you've not got a worm in your mouth?

**Nicholas**  If I knew what you meant, I'd tell you.

*A slight pause.*

I don't think you know.

**Sarah**  Go and get a book.

**Nicholas**  I don't feel like reading.

**Sarah**  Sulk then.

**Nicholas**  Sorry.

*A slight pause.*

He's rather like a child, isn't he?

**Sarah**  Who, you?

**Nicholas**  Daniel.

**Sarah** (*still reading*) Have you always been the centre of everyone's attention?

**Nicholas**  As far as I'm aware it's very much the opposite.

**Sarah**  Oh dear.

**Nicholas**  Why?

**Sarah**  I love being the centre of attention.

**Nicholas**  He said he would tell me stories. I haven't heard one yet.

**Sarah**  Then you've not been listening.

**Nicholas**  What should I have listened for?

**Sarah** (*looking up*) Mmm?

**Nicholas**  He's hard work.

**Sarah** *reads her book.*

**Nicholas** *stands up, he starts to walk back up the slope.*

**Sarah** (*putting her book aside*) It isn't you. He's like that.

**Nicholas** *stops and turns.*

And he won't thank me for gossiping. So I'm not going to.

**Nicholas**  We've walked miles together these last few days – all he's had me do is talk about myself.

**Sarah**  I'd stay. When they get back, I'd talk to Beth.

**Sarah** *picks up her book, she reads.* **Nicholas** *is still.*

You do a good impression of a statue.

**Nicholas**  I feel I'm disturbing everybody.

**Sarah**  You are.

**Nicholas** (*half smiling*) Even Mrs Melianos, she wants me out of the house.

**Nicholas** *walks back to* **Sarah**.

**Sarah** (*putting her book to one side*) He is a child. All academics are children. They're so obsessed with themselves that they never grow up. Like you.

**Nicholas**  Is that right?

**Sarah**  That's what I remember.

**Nicholas**  Were you born in Cambridge?

**Sarah**  Yes.

**Nicholas**  I think they're obsessed with their work. I'm not an academic. Not yet.

**Sarah** *lies back, she looks at the sky.*

You're very like him, Sarah.

**Nicholas** *sits down.*

**Sarah**  I try to be.

**Mimiko** *enters.*

Hello, Mimiko.

**Mimiko** *sticks his tongue out at* **Nicholas**. *He walks up the hill and sits down in the shade beneath one of the lemon trees.*

**Nicholas**  Why have they gone to Japan?

**Sarah**  Didn't he tell you?

**Nicholas**  He didn't really.

**Mimiko** *takes a small lizard from his jacket pocket. He plays with it. He lets it walk away a few inches before catching it again.*

He mumbled something about Beth being part of the American Red Cross team.

**Sarah** *sits up.*

**Sarah**  After the war when the Americans went into Japan, Beth was one of them. I don't know if it was the Red Cross – it was some sort of medical relief team. In Nagasaki she found a young girl. As far as I understand it, the girl was saved because she'd been swimming under the water in the seconds the bomb fell.

**Nicholas**  Really?

**Sarah**  She'd escaped the major force of the blast.

**Nicholas**  Go on.

**Mimiko** (*suddenly*)  This girl, she took a shine to Beth. Followed her everywhere like a mascot. These two, they became friends.

**Nicholas**  How old was she?

**Mimiko**  Little, little. Ten or nine, I think. This girl, she is one of many in the orphanage.

**Nicholas**  What happened to her?

**Mimiko**  Beth, she wants to find her again at the end of her life.

**Nicholas**  They don't know if she's alive?

**Mimiko**  That is Etsuko's story.

**Mimiko** *goes back to playing with the lizard.*

**Nicholas**  When did Beth come to England?

**Sarah**  Shortly after that.

**Nicholas**  Because of Nagasaki, and this little girl?

**Sarah**  Presumably.

**Mimiko** (*catching the lizard*)  Beth, she hated the Americans for doing that. Her country.

**Nicholas**  When did she meet your father?

**Sarah**  I don't know. Nineteen fifty something. (*Lying back, looking at the sky.*) They met at a bus stop in London.

**Nicholas**  And your father's never been to Nagasaki?

**Sarah**  No.

**Mimiko** (*holding up the lizard*)  See my lizard? He is called Daniel Howarth.

**Sarah** (*tilting her head back*)  Very nice, Mimiko. Where did you find it?

**Mimiko**  Under a stone. Shortly I let him go.

**Nicholas**  He loves her, doesn't she?

**Sarah**  You're extraordinary, Nicholas Marks.

**Nicholas**  Sorry.

**Sarah**  Extraordinarily rude. (*Lying on her elbow, looking at him.*) Are paper shops always inquisitive?

**Nicholas**  Afraid so.

**Sarah**  I think I'll ravage you. Why don't you take all your clothes off?

**Nicholas**  Stop being silly.

**Sarah**  I'm perfectly serious.

**Nicholas**  I know.

**Sarah**  Spoil sport. (*Seductively.*) Oh, please.

**Nicholas**  (*his voice rising*) No.

**Sarah**  I'll just have to imagine you then.

**Nicholas**  (*embarrassed*) Stop it.

**Sarah**  Too late. I already have.

**Nicholas** *looks embarrassed.*

Prude.

**Nicholas**  All right, I'm a prude. I'm not, of course.

**Sarah**  Sensitive little flower, aren't we?

**Nicholas**  Yes, I am, if you must know.

**Sarah**  Are paper shops sensitive, too?

**Nicholas**  Can we talk about your father, please?

**Sarah**  No, show me your willy.

**Nicholas**  Which bus stop?

**Sarah** *lies back, she looks at the sky.*

**Sarah**  What did you read at Cambridge?

**Nicholas**  Modern History.

**Sarah**  Why the paper shop then?

**Nicholas**  It fell my way.

**Sarah**  From the sky?

**Nicholas**  No, I thought it might buy me time.

**Sarah**  Did it?

**Nicholas**  Yes.

**Sarah**  What's it like?

**Nicholas**  It's like a million newsagents.

**Sarah**  Papers?

**Nicholas**  Papers and sweets. Toys. Videos.

**Sarah**  What did you want the time for?

**Nicholas**  To make decisions.

**Sarah**  What about?

**Nicholas**  Many important decisions are made too quickly.

**Sarah**  Who said?

**Nicholas**  It's only an observation.

**Sarah**  Were you clever at school?

**Nicholas**  No.

**Sarah**  I bet you were.

**Nicholas**  I worked hard, yes.

**Sarah**  Now you're doing a doctorate.

**Nicholas**  I hope to.

**Sarah**  It's brave.

**Nicholas**  Is it?

**Sarah**  Are you going to publish your thesis?

**Nicholas**  Your father made me promise I wouldn't.

**Sarah**  A promise never stopped a clever boy at school.

**Nicholas**  I'll see.

**Sarah**  Arrogant bastard.

*A slight pause.*

Have you made those important decisions?

**Nicholas**  I think so.

**Sarah**  You're covered in worms, Nicholas Marks.

*A slight pause.*

**Nicholas**  My old college had always asked me to go back. I had an open invitation. I didn't want to go before I'd thought things out. It's taken me a long time.

**Sarah** *sits up slightly. She leans on her elbows.*

**Sarah**  Why does Daniel interest you?

**Nicholas** (*thinking*)  I think academics can find themselves on the one path, that it's then hard to get off.

**Sarah**  Is that why you waited?

**Nicholas**  I witnessed that at Cambridge. The thuggery of academics. The morality of any research becomes unimportant.

**Sarah**  My father wasn't a thug.

**Nicholas**  I'm sure he wasn't.

**Sarah**  Did you expect him to be?

**Nicholas** (*thinking*)  Erm – no.

**Sarah**  He was always rather gentle.

**Nicholas**  Go on.

**Sarah**  But cut off. As if someone had wrapped him in paper. Like you.

**Nicholas** (*smiling*)  Am I like that?

**Sarah**  A bit.

**Nicholas**  Did you tease your father?

**Sarah** (*smiling*)  I learnt how to. He was also the most moral of men.

*A slight pause.*

**Nicholas**  I felt wobbly after Cambridge. I had a year in London working for a publishers, and then I opened the shop.

**Sarah**  Where?

**Nicholas**  I went home. In Skelton.

**Sarah**  Who's looking after it now?

**Nicholas**  Mrs Robson, my assistant. (*Smiling.*) I had to put all this in my letters.

**Sarah**  He always wants to know more about the other person.

**Nicholas**  Have there been many like me?

**Sarah**  No. I don't know what's changed his mind.

*A slight pause.*

**Nicholas**  Beth changed his life, didn't she?

**Sarah**  Yes.

**Mimiko** *stands up.*

**Mimiko**  I take my Daniel Howarth back to his stone. Tomorrow, I catch him again.

**Mimiko** *exits the way he came.*

**Nicholas**  Mimiko's like a puppy.

**Sarah** *stands up, she walks up the slope.*

Where are you going?

**Sarah**  Up here, to sit in the shade for a while.

**Sarah** *sits back against one of the lemon trees, leaning on it.*

(*Pointing*) There's a flying carpet, look.

**Nicholas**  What's a flying carpet?

**Sarah**  A bumblebee. He's called Axminster. He was here yesterday.

**Nicholas** *stands, he walks up the slope. He sits and leans against the other lemon tree.*

Are you gay, Nicholas.

**Nicholas**  Why d'you ask that?

**Sarah**  Just my intuition. (*Pointing.*) There's Shagpile coming out, off on a flight.

*A slight pause.*

I wouldn't mind if you were.

**Nicholas**  Is it important?

**Sarah**  Not especially.

*A slight pause.*

**Nicholas**  Where d'you live?

**Sarah**  London. Highgate. Near the cemetery.

**Nicholas**  Are you married?

**Sarah**  I used to be.

**Nicholas**  Who to?

**Sarah**  A man.

*A slight pause.*

Ask a silly question.

*A slight pause.*

I live with a painter.

**Nicholas**  An artist?

**Sarah**  Yes.

**Nicholas**  What's his name?

**Sarah**  Stuart Craig.

*A slight pause.*

He's an old man.

*A slight pause.*

He's sixty-six. (*Closing her eyes.*) Stuart's the sort of person who never gets up. He spends the entire day in his dressing-gown. (*Opening her eyes.*) Before you think he's eccentric, his paintings sell for a small fortune.

**Nicholas**  How did you meet?

**Sarah**  He stopped me in the street and asked me to change a light bulb. He's frightened of electricity.

**Nicholas**  Was he in his dressing-gown?

**Sarah**  Yes. His voice has never broken.

**Nicholas**  Why?

**Sarah**  He's resisted adulthood.

*A slight pause.*

(*Closing her eyes*.) He doesn't walk, he shuffles.

*A slight pause.*

His passion is for porcelain dogs. He's hundreds of them.

*A slight pause.*

**Nicholas**  What does he paint?

**Sarah**  Dogs.

**Sarah** *opens her eyes.*

At the moment he's painting pictures of his childhood. In Polperro. Of the fishermen he remembers, with their rowing boats. On the beach sorting fish. But they're not completely real – there's elements of fantasy. In one of them they're picking gulls from the nets, and the fish are flying. They're so, so beautiful.

*A slight pause.*

He teaches at the Slade.

**Nicholas**  How much do they sell for?

**Sarah**  Thousands now.

*A slight pause.*

I think I love him because he's like Daniel. He loves me because I accept him for what he is. I don't criticise.

*A slight pause.*

He was brought up as a girl, by his burly father.

**Nicholas**  Really?

**Sarah**  In the house, yes.

**Nicholas**  What did his mother do?

**Sarah**  Acquiesce.

*A slight pause.*

When Stuart paints himself, it's as a girl. There's always a girl and a dog in most pictures. I'm in one or two.

**Sarah** *closes her eyes.*

He used to have a spaniel called Joey. Joey was gay.

*A slight pause.*

**Nicholas** Sarah.

*A slight pause.*

Sarah?

**Nicholas** *stands up. He takes off his teeshirt. He holds it. He walks down the slope to* **Sarah**'s *bag. He puts the teeshirt on the ground and picks up the book. A photograph tumbles out.* **Nicholas** *looks at it. He puts it back between the pages.*

**Sarah** *opens her eyes.*

D'you read Evelyn Waugh?

**Sarah** Yes.

**Nicholas** *puts the book on the grass. He walks a few paces. He stands looking at the view.*

What're you looking at?

**Nicholas** Just the village. There's not a flicker.

**Sarah** I always think you can hear silence.

*Silence.*

*The burning sunlight fades to blackout.*

# Act Two

Scene One

*The hillside.*

*A week later. Tuesday, 22 May. Two o'clock in the afternoon.*

*The sun is high and bright. It is powering down once again.*

**Sarah** *enters, running. She is wearing a red bikini, and is wet from swimming. She is carrying* **Nicholas**'s *clothes, and his swimming trunks, in a bundle under her arm. She is laughing.*

**Sarah** *stops.*

**Nicholas** *enters. He, too, is wet from swimming. He is naked.*

**Nicholas**  This is not funny.

**Sarah**  Of course it is.

**Nicholas** (*taking a step forward*)  Can I have them, please.

**Sarah** *takes a step back, keeping her distance.* **Nicholas** *stops.* **Sarah** *stops.*

(*Appealingly*)  Oh, look.

**Sarah** *shakes her head.*

(*Shouting*)  Give me them now.

**Sarah**  Naughty, naughty. Ask nicely.

**Nicholas**  I've fucking well asked nicely. Where's it got me?

**Sarah** *walks to one of the lemon trees. She throws the swimming trunks right to the top.*

**Sarah**  There you are.

**Nicholas** (*furious*)  What the bloody hell's the point of that?

**Sarah** *laughs.* **Nicholas** *rushes towards her.* **Sarah** *dashes away. They stop. They are still again.*

**Sarah**  Let me count your pubic hairs. Go on. Stuart's got two thousand and seven, and his're dropping out 'cos he's an old man.

**Nicholas** (*exasperated*)  I'm not going to ask again, Sarah.

**Sarah** (*walking back to the tree*)  You've ever such a dinky bottom. (*A sing-song voice.*) Underpant time.

**Sarah** *makes as if to throw his pants into the tree.*

**Nicholas** (*his voice rising*)  Oh, don't.

*Instead she throws them to him.*

Thank you for nothing.

**Nicholas** *picks up his pants and puts them on.* **Sarah** *throws him his green teeshirt.* **Nicholas** *puts that on.* **Sarah** *is left holding his jeans. She puts them on, they are far too big for her.*

**Sarah**  If you want these, you know where they are.

**Sarah** *sits down.* **Nicholas** *goes to her. He bends down, he unfastens the jeans and takes them off. He puts them on. He sits down beside her.*

Liar. Cheat. Fibber. Runt. Imposter.

**Sarah** *takes her hand to his head. She gently runs her fingers through his hair.*

When I said last week I wouldn't mind if you were gay, what I meant was I would mind, rather a lot.

*A slight pause.*

I must've been making your life hell.

**Nicholas**  I must've made yours.

*A slight pause.*

**Sarah**  Have you a boyfriend?

**Nicholas**  Yes.

**Sarah**  Is he sexy? I bet he is.

**Nicholas**  He's quite sexy.

**Nicholas** *smiles.*

**Sarah**  On a scale of nought to ten, how sexy?

**Nicholas**  Eleven.

**Sarah**  He sounds like he's worth at least fifteen.

**Nicholas** *pulls a face.*

**Sarah** *puts her hand on his shoulders.*

Don't look like that. What's the matter?

**Nicholas**  I don't know.

**Sarah**  Have you broken up?

**Nicholas**  No. I don't know. He messes me about – trouble is I'm bloody well infatuated. It's one of those.

**Sarah**  Smack his bottom for him.

**Nicholas** *smiles.*

Where did you meet?

**Nicholas**  You'll laugh – I'm not telling you. He was a customer in the shop.

**Sarah** *massages his neck.*

He's young, too young really. I'm getting old, Sarah.

**Sarah**  You don't mean that.

**Nicholas**  No, I do.

**Sarah**  How old is he?

**Nicholas**  Eighteen. There's another guy he sees. He's bright, I enjoy his company.

**Sarah**  I shall ravage you in a minute.

**Sarah** *takes her hands away.*

**Nicholas**  I was enjoying you doing that.

**Mimiko** *enters. He looks forlorn.*

**Mimiko** (*walking up the slope*)  I have lost him.

**Sarah**  Lost who, Mimiko?

**Mimiko**  My Daniel Howarth. My lizard. (*Sitting down beneath a lemon tree.*) He is not by his stone.

**Sarah**  I'm sure he'll come back.

**Mimiko** *stretches out, he lies on his elbow.*

What are you going to do after your Ph.D?

**Nicholas** (*stretching out, lying on his elbow*)  You keep asking me that.

**Sarah** It's one of the many questions to which I never get an answer.

**Nicholas** I'd like to be a Don. Teach. Lecture. Write.

**Sarah** At Cambridge?

**Nicholas** Not necessarily. I'll go where the job is. Anywhere that will have me.

**Sarah** It's taken you all these years to decide? Like your sexuality.

**Nicholas** Something like that.

**Mimiko** *stands up. He walks towards them.*

**Mimiko** Now Nicholas will tell us his story of the farm.

**Nicholas** Oh God.

**Mimiko** *sits down.*

It's too hot.

**Sarah** (*gently kicking* **Nicholas**) Don't miss out the grisly bits.

**Mimiko** Grisly bits.

**Nicholas** There isn't any story. I wasn't brought up on a farm. Your father seems to have found great delight in telling everyone I was. Even Mrs Melianos tried to ask. The phrase book wasn't bloody adequate.

**Sarah** (*kicking him*) Get on with it.

**Nicholas** (*quickly*) Bl-bl-bl-bl-bl-bl-bl-bl-bl-bl-bl-bl-bl-bl-bl-bl-bl-bl-bl-bl- (*Getting quicker.*) bl-bl-bl-bl-bl-bl-bl-bl-bl-bl-bl-bl-bl-bl-bl

**Mimiko** It is because he has not a cigarette.

**Mimiko** *takes a packet of Greek cigarettes from his jacket pocket.*

**Nicholas** I told you it yesterday.

**Mimiko** *puts a cigarette in* **Nicholas**'s *mouth. He lights it with a match.*

**Sarah** Not that one. Another one.

**Nicholas** I don't know any more stories.

**Mimiko** Tell us about you this time.

**Nicholas** Oh, look.

**Mimiko** Yes, yes, you must.

**Nicholas** About me? This isn't fair.

**Nicholas** *sits up.*

**Mimiko** Nicholas's story.

**Nicholas** My aunt and uncle had the farm. At a village called Castleton, near Skelton, which was where I was brought up and where my home is now.

*A cloud passes in front of the sun. The sun goes in.*

It was a hill farm. Quite poor and not at all grand. I used to spend my summers there.

**Mimiko** This we got yesterday.

**Sarah** *kicks* **Nicholas.**

**Nicholas** I didn't very much like the farm because I was an only child, and had no one to play with. Sob, sob.

**Mimiko** What is this sob sob?

**Sarah** *kicks* **Nicholas.**

**Nicholas** My aunt and uncle were very old-fashioned where children were concerned. But I went because my mother wanted me to.

**Mimiko** *nods.*

My mother was old-fashioned. Very, very. More than my aunt and uncle. I'm what's known as a bastard, Mimiko.

**Mimiko** (*nodding*) Bastard.

**Nicholas** But not the swear word kind. A bastard in the sense that I don't know who my father is. I've never been able to find him. (*To* **Sarah.**) When my mother died I looked through her papers, but there was nothing. All I know is that my mother never worked, but we always had money. Some money. Not a lot. But enought. (*To* **Mimiko.**) If my mother were being truthful, I think she'd say she never wanted a child. Don't get me wrong, she wasn't unkind. It was just that she didn't know how to talk to a small boy.

**Nicholas** *drags on the cigarette.*

(*Looking between them*)  We lived a life of flowered wallpaper, heavy curtains, and silences by the coal fire. Me with my homework on my knee. At the grammar school. Working for all I was worth.

**Mimiko**  This is the best so far.

**Nicholas**  When she died I discovered fifteen thousand pounds in a bank account. With that, I bought the shop.

**Mimiko**  I prefer this story of a bastard.

**Nicholas** *offers* **Mimiko** *the cigarette.*

You keep it, it is a present for you. Smoke it, and you find your father.

**Nicholas**  I don't want to. It's not a story about longing.

**Mimiko**  You see. One day he will come through the mist. He will say to you, 'Son, I have found you.' Everyone will be happy.

**Nicholas**  You're an optimist, Mimiko.

**Mimiko**  What else is there to be in this life? I ask you? Pessimism is only for those who congratulate themselves on their own pessimism. Pessimism is for those who only love themselves.

**Nicholas** *drags on the cigarette.*

We must have hope. Without hope, what are we? We are a people revelling in misery. I am young, I have told you. (*Pointing.*) You see the highest hill on our island?

**Nicholas** *looks.*

There is your father. Go to him.

**Nicholas** *looks back to* **Mimiko**.

I, too, have no father. I have no mother. I live like a dog on the edge of things. But that is best. (*Smiling.*) I tell you my story and not smoke cigarette. My health is better.

**Nicholas** *and* **Sarah** *smile.*

We Greeks have many stories. I tell good?

**Sarah**  Yes.

**Mimiko**  You think also?

**Nicholas**  Yes.

**Mimiko**  Then I am pleased. (*Proudly.*) I am a storyteller like old Lekas.

**Nicholas**  Who's he?

**Mimiko**  Old Lekas is the best storyteller on our island.

*The cloud goes. The sun comes out.*

Old Lekas is very old. One hundred and fifty at least. (*Pointing.*) He live beyond the hill of your father. Old Lekas, he is an informer in this war, when the Germans are here. Our fathers, my father, they cut his tongue out for this. Daniel, he call him his guru.

**Mimiko** *waves his hands through the air.*

Like this they tell stories. I have seen.

**Sarah**  They've invented a sign language.

**Mimiko**  It is so. They talk in silence, these two. This man is a sage. He has no tongue. I have seen them.

**Nicholas**  Why didn't you tell me?

**Sarah**  Daniel keeps him to himself. Mimiko hasn't met him, either.

**Mimiko**  Yes, yes, you woman. I sneak behind Daniel one day on his walk. See where he go. (*Pointing.*) We go over the hill. A long walk. I sneak for half a day. They sit outside his hut, and smoke. All the time, smoking. This going on.

**Mimiko** *demonstrates the sign language more accurately. His face becomes very expressive, like a clown, as he touches it with his fingers, very quickly, in various different places.*

It make me want to laugh. I laugh so much I scare up the birds. They see me. I am drawn to them. Old Lekas, he fetch wine. We drink like three fuck fishes. This man he is a thousand years old, for his wisdom. This man, he is the history of our country.

**Nicholas**  Is this true?

**Mimiko**  You think I am a liar?

**Nicholas**  No. What do they talk about?

**Mimiko**  It is about this big exploding bomb which Daniel make. It go bang many times.

*He demonstrates the bomb going off with his voice and hands.*

Bang. Bang. Bang. A big firework for the world. This bomb, it is so big it create new stars in the sky. (*Awe in his voice.*) It is as powerful as the very sun. (*After a moment's pause.*) Daniel, says to Lekas, he is not a strong man now. The making of the sun has weakened him. (*After a moment's pause.*) Old Lekas, he is the one who understand this new universe. He is history. He forgive Daniel. That is why he and Daniel talk.

*A slight pause.*

These two traitors only see each other. When he die, I take his place. I become like the land of Greece. My blood become soil. My heart a mountain. I sit at the top, a wise man. At the moment I am young. I wait for the wisdom of the history of my country.

*A slight pause.*

When I have my lizard, I hear you say, you study history?

**Nicholas**  Yes.

**Mimiko**  Daniel, he say history is not the study of facts. It is the study of ourselves. Of our stories. The stories we tell each other. When we understand our stories, then we are in a position to look at the facts. This is how we learn the whys and wherefores. From Daniel, I begin to see this. It is only the genius who understands and does not lie.

**Nicholas**  Yes.

**Mimiko**  You lie?

**Nicholas**  Sometimes.

**Mimiko**  But of course, the truth is savage. Real truth, make real changes in our lives. Daniel, he strive to be a man.

*A slight pause.*

Is this why you work in the paper shop? To find the truth?

**Nicholas**  *smiles.*

And now you leave your Mrs Robson? It is a good thing. You give her the shop. That act of generosity make her think about her life.

**Mimiko** *stands up. He walks up the slope to one of the lemon trees. He sits down.*

*A slight pause.*

**Nicholas**  Have you been to school, Mimiko?

**Mimiko**  What are schools? They are useless.

**Sarah** (*lying on her side, on her elbow*)  Yes, you have.

**Mimiko**  I go for a few years. Like Daniel, I prefer stories. Schools, they do not listen. Too much teaching.

**Nicholas** *lies on his side, on his elbow.* **Mimiko** *leans back against the tree.*

*The sun goes in.*

The weather, it is sticky today.

**Sarah** *lies on her back, she looks at the sky.*

**Sarah**  Is it going to rain?

**Mimiko**  Later, maybe. This is why my lizard is not by his stone. He go underground.

**Nicholas** *lies on his back. The three of them are still.*

*A pause.*

*A light change: the overcast summer sunlight slowly fades. A darker light is left from a rain-filled sky.*
*Time has passed. Two hours later.*

*A pause.*

*A bee-eater calls from one of the lemon trees.*
**Mimiko** *stands up, he goes to the other tree. He looks into it, searching with his eyes.*
*The bee-eater calls.*

**Mimiko** *whistles, imitating the bird's call. He stretches out the flat of his hand.*
**Nicholas** *stands up.*
**Mimiko** *whistles.* **Nicholas** *walks towards him.*

Move slowly, please.

**Nicholas** *walks carefully. He joins* **Mimiko**.

This is my friend the bee-eater. See?

**Nicholas** (*quietly*) Yes.

**Mimiko** Sometimes he will land on my palm. Not today. It is because of the storm. (*Suddenly moving his hand, following the flight of the bird.*) There he go, look. I follow him. It will rain soon.

**Mimiko** *follows the bee-eater. He exits.*

**Nicholas** *watches him go. He takes his wrist-watch from his pocket and puts it on.*

**Sarah** *still hasn't moved.*

**Nicholas** *walks to the beehive. He looks at it.*

**Sarah** It's empty.

**Nicholas** I wondered why we hadn't been stung to death.

**Sarah** *rolls onto her stomach, so that she can see him.*

**Sarah** He's extraordinary.

**Nicholas** Mimiko?

**Sarah** Yes. I was a teacher.

**Nicholas** *smiles.*

What're you smiling at?

**Nicholas** What did you teach?

**Sarah** Infants.

**Nicholas** Have you a child, Sarah?

**Sarah** Worms, worms, and more worms.

**Nicholas** A photograph fell out of your book.

**Sarah** *jumps up. She walks towards him.*

**Sarah** Lie down, please.

**Nicholas**, *warily, lies down.* **Sarah** *sits astride him.*

**Nicholas** You'll crush my rib-cage.

**Sarah** *pushes up his teeshirt. She 'hoovers' his navel – the sound with her voice, the actions with her hand.*

What you doing?

**Sarah**  Hoovering your belly-button.

*She stops. She pulls his teeshirt down.*

Yes. She lives with her father. I was the one who walked out.

**Nicholas**  For Stuart?

**Sarah**  Did you ever imagine a light bulb could change your life?

**Nicholas**  No.

**Sarah**  I tried with Philip.

**Nicholas**  Stop pretending.

**Sarah**  No, I did – I tried really hard. Meals on the table. Slippers by the fire. Not quite, but almost. Philip's remarried. She's a terrific home. (*Smiling.*) I still hate him.

**Nicholas** *smiles.*

No, Philip's very conventional. I discovered I wasn't, that's all.

**Nicholas**  How often d'you see her?

**Sarah**  Half of each school holiday. One weekend in two. They live in Bristol – so not as often as I'd wish. People said how could I walk out and leave a child.

**Nicholas**  It hurts you, doesn't it?

**Sarah**  D'you like to think of people being hurt?

**Nicholas**  Don't be silly.

*A slight pause.*

**Sarah**  As a matter-of-fact, it is hell. Fucking hell, Nicholas.

**Nicholas**  I'm sorry.

**Sarah** *jumps up, she runs away down the slope. She stops.* **Nicholas** *stands up. He walks to her. He comes up behind her and puts his hands on her shoulders.*

**Sarah**  I came here to talk to my dad. He's so brick wallish now, it's impossible. If only he'd talk to me – tell me what's wrong.

**Nicholas** I know.

**Sarah** Do you? No, you don't. I came here to talk about Stuart.

**Nicholas** *puts his arm around her waist.*

I'd been overseeing an exhibition. I came back and he was lying on the floor in his studio. He was sort of crumpled. A dreary stroke.

**Nicholas** How long had you been together?

**Sarah** Five and a half years. (*Looking at him.*) He died just as I got him to the hospital. Six weeks ago. The house is a tip. It's odd, because I've been finding things ever since. Things I didn't know about. I found a pile of uncashed cheques under a carpet I pulled up. Hundreds of old letters. And letters from your mother in Skelton. About you.

**Nicholas** *looks down.*

About how you were doing at school. About how she needed more money for pencils. It's a big house, he kept everything.

**Nicholas** *walks away a pace. He looks at her.*

**Nicholas** Why, Sarah?

**Sarah** Why what?

**Nicholas** These games?

**Sarah** No. Mimiko was right.

**Nicholas** (*shaking his head*) It couldn't be. How?

**Sarah** I don't know how.

**Nicholas** How could they have met? How?

**Sarah** I don't know how.

**Nicholas** It's preposterous.

**Sarah** It's not.

*A slight pause.*

**Nicholas** Completely and absolutely ridiculous.

**Sarah** I'll show you the letters. In London.

**Nicholas** Tell me how they could possibly have met?

**Sarah** I don't know that.

*A slight pause.*

It suddenly hit me.

**Nicholas** When?

**Sarah** Just now, when you told Mimiko. I know your mother's name.

**Nicholas** Telling stories is one thing. (*Shaking his head.*) No, Sarah.

**Sarah** It's the truth.

**Nicholas** Oh, I don't know. What the hell do I know about anything.

*A slight pause.*

Tell me her name?

**Sarah** Joyce. I know it's right.

**Nicholas** *looks down.*

I found all sorts of paintings I didn't know about.

**Nicholas** (*looking up*) Is it true, what you said about him?

**Sarah** Yes.

**Nicholas** His being brought up as a girl.

**Sarah** Yes.

**Nicholas** Well, we'll never know, will we?

**Sarah** No.

**Nicholas** *walks up the slope. He stops and turns.*

Was your mother's name Joyce?

**Nicholas** Yes.

**Sarah** *walks to him. They embrace. They sway from side to side.*

**Sarah** I'm sorry.

**Nicholas** What for? I'm sorry for you. Losing someone that you loved. That's nice. You're nice and warm.

**Sarah** You've been terrific this last week.

**Nicholas**  Have I?

**Sarah**  Letting me abuse you.

**Nicholas**  I got used to it. I suppose technically we might be related.

**Sarah**  We were never married. Stuart wouldn't. He had a thing about it. He wouldn't have children, either. Because of what his father did.

**Nicholas**  It all makes sense, in a way.

**Sarah**  Stories do.

**Daniel** *and* **Beth** *enter.*

**Daniel** *is wearing his suit with his white shirt.* **Beth** *is wearing a dark purple tweed skirt and a white blouse. They have sandals on their feet.*

**Daniel** *and* **Beth** *look well and refreshed.*

**Nicholas** *sees them. He and* **Sarah** *part.*

We weren't expecting you for ages. When did you get back?

**Daniel**  Half an hour ago, didn't we?

**Beth** *smiles.*

**Sarah**  Have you had a good time?

**Beth**  Wonderful.

**Daniel** (*walking forward a pace*)  We'll tell you, pet.

**Beth**  Some sadness – to be among the people of the city and know what they lived through.

**Daniel**  The Peace Memorial itself is not very nice. Is it?

**Beth**  No, it's rather ugly. A huge bronze buddah. His right hand is held to the sky from where the bomb fell, and his left to the ground, holding back the forces of evil.

**Daniel**  His eyes are closed in prayer.

**Beth**  We spent a morning there, talking.

**Sarah**  So you're glad you went?

**Daniel**  I'm glad, pet, yes.

**Beth** (*walking to* **Daniel**. *Smiling*) It's been the journey of my life. I think you got more from it than me, didn't you?

**Daniel** Are you going to tell them?

**Daniel** *and* **Beth** *smile at one another.*

**Beth** I wish you both could have seen her. (*Taking* **Daniel**'s *hand*.) Wasn't she lovely?

**Sarah** Come on then.

**Beth** (*a beaming smile*) I might even have recognised her, Sarah.

**Daniel** She saw Beth straight away.

**Beth** There she was. Standing there. In her school corridor.

**Daniel** Etsuko nearly had a heart attack.

**Sarah** You did find her?

**Daniel** We thought it might take us weeks and weeks.

**Beth** We found her on the first afternoon.

**Sarah** What's she like?

**Daniel** We'll tell you.

**Beth** She's alive and well. She's married – called Mrs Oogushi.

**Daniel** She's a teacher in a primary school.

*It starts to rain. It rains hard. The sound echoes off the baked earth.*

Let's shelter under the trees.

**Beth** *and* **Daniel** *go to one tree.*

**Sarah** *and* **Nicholas** *to the other.*
*The sky is darkening.*
*They talk over the rain.*

**Beth** She's two children of her own. We took them all out to dinner.

**Daniel** Tell them the best bit.

**Beth** I was saving that.

**Daniel** Tell them.

**Sarah** What?

**Daniel**  Tell them, or I will.

**Beth**  On our last afternoon there, she invited us back to the school. Her children performed a play for us.

**Daniel**  It was beautiful, Sarah.

**Nicholas** *is looking at the sky.*
*It is now very dark. Almost black.*

**Beth**  About her life. They'd been performing it the week before, for parents. They did it again especially for us.

*A bright flash of lightning.*

*This is immediately followed by an enormous clap of thunder. It rumbles and shakes the ground.*

*It rains harder. The sound echoes loudly off the baked earth. They have to shout.*

**Daniel**  (*talking* **Beth** *with him away from the tree*) It's an electric storm. Come out. It's dangerous under there.

**Sarah**  What?

**Daniel**  Don't stand under the trees.

**Nicholas**  (*walking from the tree*) Your father's right.

**Daniel**  (*pointing to the sky*) It's right overhead.

**Nicholas**  Sarah.

**Daniel**  (*beckoning her*) Come out, love.

**Sarah**  We'll get wet.

*A flash of lightning. It strikes above* **Sarah**'s *head.*

*The lemon tree splits in half, but doesn't fall completely.*

**Sarah** *is still, rigid.*
*A thunder clap echoes and rumbles.*

**Nicholas**  (*shouting*) Sarah.

**Sarah** *falls back a few inches. She is left propped up, standing, against the broken tree.*

**Nicholas** *rushes towards her.*

**Daniel**  (*rushing himself*) Don't touch her, Nicholas. (*Joining him.*) Leave it a second.

*They wait a second.*

**Daniel** *picks her up. He carries her in his arms away from the tree. A flash of lightning.* **Daniel** *puts her down.*

**Nicholas** *kneels.* **Beth** *kneels. She takes* **Sarah**'s *pulse. A thunder clap echoes.*

**Beth** (*calmly, to* **Nicholas**) Push on her chest when I say.

**Beth** *takes a deep breath, she holds* **Sarah**'s *nose and breathes into her mouth.*

Now.

**Nicholas** *pushes on* **Sarah**'s *chest. They repeat this. It seems to go on for ages. Occasionally* **Beth** *takes* **Sarah**'s *pulse.*

**Daniel** *watches.*

**Beth** *takes* **Sarah**'s *pulse.* **Beth** *changes position. With her hands she hammers into* **Sarah**'s *body above her heart.* **Sarah** *jumps under the weight of the blows.*

*The rain is beginning to quieten a little.* **Beth** *takes* **Sarah**'s *pulse.*

**Daniel**  Is there anything I can do, love?

**Beth**  I don't think so.

**Beth** *hammers again. Her hair is falling out of place. She is beginning to breathe deeply, having to catch her breath.*

*The rain is quietening.*

**Nicholas**  What if I breathe into her mouth?

**Beth**  Try it.

**Nicholas** *breathes into* **Sarah**'s *mouth.* **Beth** *continues with her hammering.*

*A bright ray of sunlight slants down through a hole in the clouds. The rain is quietening.* **Beth** *takes* **Sarah**'s *pulse.*

(*Breathing deeply*) She's dead, I'm afraid.

**Daniel** *puts his hands on* **Beth**'s *shoulders.*

I don't know what else I can do.

*The rain stops.*

*Silence.*

**Nicholas**  She can't just be dead.

*Silence.*

*The bright ray of sunlight slowly fades to blackout.*


Scene Two

*The hillside.*

*Four days later. Saturday, 26 May. Ten o'clock in the morning.*

*The sky is clear. A dazzlingly bright sunlight is burning down.*

**Clare** *enters, running by one of the lemon trees. She runs down the slope and stops.*

**Clare** *is twelve and, if anything, looks slightly young for her age. With her short blonde hair, and slight thin frame, she is the spitting image of* **Sarah**. *She is wearing sandals, knee-length white socks, and a white, short-sleeved dress. A pause.*

**Beth** *enters by the tree, slightly breathless. She is wearing her flowered dress.*

**Beth**  You chased ahead of me.

**Clare** *turns to* **Beth**.

**Clare**  Is this the place, Gran?

**Beth** (*walking down*)  Yes, love.

**Clare** *looks about.*

**Clare**  Was that the tree?

**Beth**  Yes.

**Clare**  It will be a sad tree forever, won't it, Gran?

**Beth**  Unfortunately, love, it will.

**Beth** *takes* **Clare**'s *hand.*

**Clare**  D'you know how many letters Mummy sent me from Greece?

**Beth**  No?

**Clare**  Three. I gave the stamps to a boy at my school.

**Beth**  Did you?

**Clare**  Is the funeral tomorrow?

**Beth**  Yes, love.

**Clare**  When I was eight my guinea-pig died.

**Beth**  Did he?

**Clare**  He was a her.

**Beth**  That's right, I remember now. Sally, wasn't it?

**Clare**  *nods.*

**Clare**  We buried Sally in the garden.

**Beth**  Mummy will be buried here, won't she?

**Clare**  *nods.*

**Clare**  (*after a moment's pause*)  I've got gerbils now.

*A slight pause.*

**Beth**  You just wanted to have a quick look, didn't you? Shall we go back?

**Clare**  Gran?

**Beth**  Yes, love?

**Clare**  Why did Mummy die, Gran?

**Beth**  *thinks for a moment.*

**Beth**  Mummy was unlucky, wasn't she?

**Clare**  *nods.*

Mummy lives in our memories of her, Clare.

**Clare**  *nods.*

You're being a brave girl.

**Clare**  Daddy wasn't sure if I should come. I wanted to.

**Beth**  It was a long way, wasn't it, on your own?

**Clare**  *nods.*

D'you want to find Grandpa? And Nicholas? Or d'you want to spend more time here.

**Clare** *nods.*

Which?

**Clare**  Find Grandpa and Nicholas.

*They walk towards the beach.* **Clare** *stops. She turns and looks at the hillside.* **Beth** *turns.*

**Clare**  Grandpa told me when Mummy was my age – you know what she did?

**Beth**  No?

**Clare**  Well, you know how you put a book above the door? And when the person comes in it lands on their head? Mummy put a pound of flour, eggs, some butter, some sugar, and some cherries. Grandpa came in. By the time it hit the floor it was a cherry cake.

*They walk towards the beach.*

**Beth**  I think your Grandpa's teasing you, Clare.

**Clare**  I'm going to tease him when I think of something.

**Clare** *skips off.* **Beth** *follows her.*

*The bright sunlight fades to blackout.*


Scene Three

*The beach at Panormos.*

*The sand rises in a steady, even incline from the sea at the bottom to the high-tide line at the top. There are a few pieces of sea debris on this line. The sand is almost white. To one side a whitish rock rises from the sand. Painted on it in white, so that it is barely readable, is 'No Nude Sunbathing'.*

*Saturday, 26 May. A few seconds later.*
*The same dazzlingly bright sun is burning down.*

*Spread out on the sand at the top of the slope, close to the rock, is a large bath towel.* **Daniel**'s *clothes are lying in a heap beside it.*

**Nicholas** *is standing at the bottom of the slope beside the sea. He is wearing his cord trousers and his check shirt. His shoes and socks are beside him on the sand. He is looking out to sea.*

**Mimiko** *enters along the high-tide line. He walks towards* **Nicholas**.

**Mimiko**  Beth is with Clare. They go to the place where it happened. I do not like to go with them.

*He stands beside* **Nicholas**.

Her body, it is in a coffin now, in the cool of our church. My people, we pay our respects, too. It is good that she be buried here.

**Mimiko** *is looking at the sea*.

How is he today?

**Nicholas**  He seems better. I think Clare being here has helped.

**Mimiko**  He blame himself for everything, this man.

**Nicholas**  I know.

**Mimiko**  We have to tell him, the storm, it is not his fault. Look how he swim like the fish, despite his age.

*A slight pause*.

We first meet when I am seven years old, Nicholas.

**Nicholas** *smiles*.

You stay for the funeral?

**Nicholas**  Yes. I'm going on Monday.

**Mimiko**  To write your thesis?

**Nicholas**  I shall try.

**Mimiko**  On Daniel?

**Nicholas**  No. On chance. How chance has shaped history.

**Mimiko**  Is this a change for you?

**Nicholas**  It was always part of my thinking. But, yes.

**Mimiko**  I understand chance.

**Nicholas**  Do you?

**Mimiko**  It is everyday around us. It involve us all.

**Nicholas** *smiles*.

I speak the obvious thing sometimes.

**Nicholas**  Will you ever come to England?

**Mimiko** *shrugs.*

**Mimiko**  It is in the future. Who can tell?

**Nicholas**  If you do, write to me, let me know.

**Mimiko**  I will. What is your one thought of our island.

**Nicholas** (*after thinking for a second*)  It has a freedom.

**Daniel** *enters from the sea. He is wearing a pair of baggy, old-fashioned swimming trunks. He shuffles to his towel.*

**Daniel**  You should have gone in, Nicholas.

**Daniel** *picks up the towel and starts to dry himself.*

**Mimiko** (*looking at the sea*)  Petros is out there, Daniel.

**Daniel**  Yes, I saw him. He's still rowing back.

**Mimiko** (*to* **Nicholas**)  Petros is one of our fishermen, in his boat. He is slowest. Daniel, he likes the slowest.

**Daniel**  Petros is a wise man, Mimiko.

**Mimiko** (*raising his voice*)  It is the wise man who move slowly, eh Daniel?

**Daniel** (*realising* **Mimiko** *is teasing him*)  Yes.

**Mimiko** (*to* **Nicholas**)  He have time to understand.

**Mimiko** *screws his finger into his temple.*

Petros want a motor. Then he get his breakfast.

**Daniel**  Push off. *Egho thelo milo Nicholas.*

**Mimiko**  You wish to talk together.

**Mimiko** *walks up the slope, to the hightide line.*

Before I go, Daniel – may I take Clare fishing one evening? I have my rods.

**Daniel**  I'm sure she'd love that. Speak to Beth.

**Mimiko**  Thank you.

**Daniel** (*affectionately*) *Efharisto.*

**Mimiko** *goes the way he came.*

(*Holding the towel.*) Yes, I like an early morning dip. Sarah was a brave swimmer.

*He continues to dry himself.*

I get jealous of Mimiko. His youth, his time. When he was little we used to make things up together. Oh, silly things.

*He is still. He holds the towel.*

I hope I've not hurt him. Or spoiled him in any way.

**Nicholas**  No, you've done a good job.

**Daniel**  I never found the space for my own students. Pity. Will you?

**Nicholas**  I'd hope to.

**Daniel**  Mmm.

**Nicholas**  What?

**Daniel**  Oh, your hope may not be enough. Those cloisters have their own power to mislead. Perhaps I'm telling you what you already know?

**Nicholas**  (*smiling*)  A bit.

**Daniel**  It never hurts us, does it?

**Nicholas**  What?

**Daniel**  Being told we're right.

**Nicholas**  (*smiling*)  No.

**Daniel**  If I get self-indulgent, please stop me.

*He spreads his towel on the sand.*

No, I've never asked to be liked for what I've done. I don't think it's admirable. Mmm? Do you?

**Nicholas**  Yes, I do think it's admirable. I'm sorry to surprise you. What is not, is the pity and disgust.

**Daniel**  No, no.

**Nicholas**  It's an arrogance that allows you to take the blame.

**Daniel**  Of course you're right.

**Nicholas**  Then stop.

**Daniel**  I have tried to change. I've just never been very successful.

*A slight pause.*

No, there is no whole or absolute truth. Not in what I say.

*A slight pause.*

I am the same person, Nicholas, that I was thirty years ago. I could build those bombs again. The 'I' is important. I led the programme. There were others who have some comfort. You see, if I don't take the blame, all I begin to do is justify. Because, by God, they were exciting times.

*A slight pause.*

Forgive me. Already I'm justifying.

*He puts his finger to his lips.*

Sssh. Mmm?

**Nicholas**  Is that why you've remained silent?

*A slight pause.*

Why did you agree to see me?

**Daniel**  I hoped you might understand my paradoxes.

**Nicholas**  Would you – now – work on the programme?

**Daniel**  No, of course I wouldn't. What I'm saying, is that I still have the desire for that excitement. I realise, intellectually, how appalling that is, or must seem – emotionally, I'm not sure. Because that's what I want. (*After a moment's pause.*) No, I am sure, it's equally appalling.

*A slight pause.*

What is history, Nicholas?

**Nicholas**  I'm begining to feel it's nothing but a series of random chances.

**Daniel**  I'm not a historian, but it seems to me we look at history in the wrong way. We have to look at ourselves first. At our own stories. When we stop repeating our own failings, and take responsibility for our actions, maybe we have a chance.

*A slight pause.*

I have tried to take responsibility for mine.

*A slight pause.*

I repeat, I'm not asking to be liked for what I've done. If that is self-pitying, so be it.

**Nicholas** *walks up the sand to the high-tide line.*

**Nicholas**  What about your own history?

**Daniel** (*picking up his jacket*)  My father was a docker. A unionist, an agitator.

*He takes a packet of cigarettes and a box of matches from the pocket. He puts the jacket down.*

When they sacked him I must have been in my early teens. You were right, we did go without shoes for a while.

**Daniel** *lights a cigarette.*

My father was a stoic. A great educationalist. He read the Co-op library from cover to cover. When he died there were over a thousand people at his funeral. There's a school named after him in Manchester. The William Howarth School.

*He throws the cigarette packet and the box of matches onto his jacket.*

He taught us that learning meant dignity. He was wrong, of course. How I wish I'd been a plumber, or an electrician.

**Nicholas**  Do you feel you've abused that?

**Daniel**  What?

**Nicholas**  That dignity.

**Daniel**  Oh, I think I have, don't you?

*He puffs on his cigarette.*

When I left Manchester Grammar School I worked for a company which specialised in making laboratory equipment. I was nineteen, twenty, twenty-two. Eventually, kindly, they saw me through Cambridge. Can you imagine how exciting those years were? Mingling with the best, beating them.

*He puffs on his cigarette.*

To use your analogy, the path of atomic physics seemed clear. I just walked along it. No, strode arrogantly. I envy you your intelligence.

**Nicholas**  How much of an idea had you of what the research might mean?

**Daniel**  We knew it was important. Obviously, we did. How much d'you ever know the consequences of something which isn't yet finished? The pattern comes later. We were aware it had implications, yes we were. And we knew research of a very similar kind was going on all over Europe. And America.

**Daniel**'s *hand is shaking slightly.* He *puffs on his cigarette.*

I was a junior then, don't forget. It wasn't until the war – the war escalated the whole bloody damn thing. When the government finally realised what had been going on – well, that was it, it was out of our hands. Correspondence with Europe stopped. The Americans moved into Los Alamos.

**Daniel**'s *hand is shaking.*

In nineteen forty-five we were frightened that Hitler would get there first.

**Daniel** *puffs on his cigarette. He is speaking more quietly.*

And after the war, well – for the same reasons we'd been frightened of Germany, we were now scared stiff of the Russians. For all we knew, Russia already had an atom bomb.

*A slight pause.*

So I went on working, Nicholas.

*A slight pause.*

Most of my real work was done on the hydrogen bomb in the fifties. Though that's not important. It was too late by then. As you should know, knowledge has its own momentum. It's unstoppable. That's what my father didn't understand.

**Nicholas**  I have read somewhere that you thought you were philosophers.

**Daniel**  If philosophy is the study of the ultimate nature of existence. Then we were meddling with something at the very heart of that – the atom. The atom had been the one certain law of the universe. To split it, split all laws.

**Daniel** *picks up the packet of cigarettes.*

I think there is still one law I still respect. One truth.

*He lights a second cigarette from the first.*

You see, Nicholas – unlike the atom – knowledge can never be destroyed. That's what hurts me.

*He stubs out the first cigarette.*

What I've left behind, the world has to find a way of coping with. And that's fine if you think about it for a few weeks, or a few months, or a few years. But think about it for centuries.

*A slight pause.*

**Nicholas** I'm sorry.

**Daniel** *walks to the edge of the sea.*

**Daniel** Oh, I don't blame you.

**Nicholas** *walks down the sand to the sea. They are standing some distance apart.*

You have to remember we were dealing with the unknown. Daily. Day in, day out. I think now the word philosophy implies that one does some good. We didn't.

*He puffs on his cigarette.*

I led the programme throughout the fifties.

**Nicholas** And you left because of Beth?

**Daniel** That's right.

*He puffs on his cigarette.*

To say I fell in love, sounds simplistic – but it's the truth.

*A slight pause.*

I fell in love with her story. Of her, a young woman in that desolate city. And a girl.

**Daniel**'s *hand is shaking again. He puffs on his cigarette.*

Stories change our lives, if only we'd listen to them.

**Daniel** *walks up the sand to the high-tide line. He turns and looks at the sea.*

I stood in front of Etsuko and all I could do was apologize.

**Daniel**'s *eyes flood with tears.* **Nicholas** *goes to him. He puts his hands on* **Daniel**'s *shoulders.*

**Nicholas**  It was the wrong time to ask a lot of questions.

**Daniel**  No, no.

*They fall into a hug.*

And now Sarah. What appalling self-pity.

**Nicholas**  It's honest.

*A pause.*

You feeling better?

*They break the hug.* **Nicholas** *takes a handkerchief from his pocket.*

**Daniel**  Is it clean?

**Daniel** *takes it. He dries his eyes with it.*

**Nicholas**  It isn't brilliantly clean. I only brought the one.

**Daniel**  It's a hanky.

*A slight pause.*

**Daniel** *stands with the handkerchief in his hand.*

You are staying for Sarah's funeral?

**Nicholas**  Yes, of course I am.

**Daniel** (*holding up the hanky*)  D'you want it back?

**Nicholas**  Keep it.

*A slight pause.*

**Daniel**'s *eyes fill with tears again. They hug.*

Eh.

*A pause.*

Eh.

*A slight pause.*

Eh.

*They break the hug.*

**Daniel**  Oh dear.

**Daniel** *dries his eyes on the handkerchief.* **Nicholas** *wipes away a tear, with his thumb, from his own eye.*

Have I got you at it?

**Daniel** *bends down, he stubs out the cigarette.*

What are you going to do?

**Nicholas**  Go home. Think.

**Daniel** *walks down the sand.*

*They are both looking at the sea.*

**Daniel**  If I can find the courage – I may go back myself, Nicholas.

**Nicholas**  You should.

**Daniel**  D'you think? Is it worth the chance?

**Nicholas**  Yes.

**Daniel**  D'you know what I most regret – is the loss of innocence.

**Nicholas** *walks down the sand to the sea.*

If you look at the sea. Oh, I don't know. Every drop of it contains some sort of story. (*Looking at* **Nicholas**.) Is open to influence. If only from the wind. The tide comes in and out. Every drop of it's been somewhere.

*He looks at the sea.*

What every story has is a threat hanging around it.

*A slight pause.*

I don't know if we'll ever put that right.

*The bright sunlight fades to blackout.*


Scene Four

*The beach.*

*Three days later. Monday, 29 May. Nine o'clock in the evening.*

*The sky is bright and starless. Only a full moon can be seen, casting a shadow from the rock. It lights the beach with a rich glow.*

*At the base of the rock are the dying embers of a small fire. Above the fire is a metal grate which has been used for grilling fish.*

**Beth** *enters from the village, walking by the sea. She is wearing her flowered dress and a cardigan.*

**Daniel** *enters behind her. He is wearing his suit and his white shirt.*

**Beth** *stops and turns.* **Daniel** *holds out his hand.* **Beth** *takes it.*

**Daniel**  The village were wonderful, don't you think?

**Beth**  Marvellous. I hadn't quite realised how much they'd taken Sarah to their hearts.

**Daniel** *brushes his finger along her cheek.*

**Daniel**  How is it?

**Beth**  Not too bad. (*Smiling.*) So far, so good.

**Daniel**  You will say, won't you, if you want anything?

**Beth**  I want nothing.

**Daniel**  I know, but you should.

**Mimiko** *enters from along the beach. He is carrying two small fish, one in each hand.*

**Mimiko** (*going to the fire*)  Clare says you are to have these. We've had ours.

**Mimiko** *puts the fish on the metal grate.*

**Beth**  How many have you caught?

**Mimiko**  Clare's caught twenty-seven. I've caught six.

**Daniel**  That's well done.

**Mimiko**  I don't know how she does it. (*Walking back the way he came.*) Don't forget, you are to turn them over in seven minutes.

**Beth**  Tell Clare it's nearly her bedtime.

**Mimiko**  She says not to be silly, it's not nearly her bedtime.

**Mimiko** *goes.*

**Daniel** That told you.

**Beth** (*smiling*) I'm sure it won't hurt her, for once.

**Daniel** (*smiling*) I don't know how she does it, either.

**Beth** It's easier for children. Clare is what she is.

**Daniel** Yes.

**Beth** She had a good cry with me this morning.

**Daniel** *puts his arm around her waist.*

**Daniel** When did we meet?

**Beth** Don't be an old goat.

**Daniel** (*smiling*) I felt lucky that day.

*A slight pause.*

It doesn't seem that long ago. Does it to you?

**Beth** Not really.

**Daniel** It's twenty-five years, you know.

**Beth** It isn't. (*After thinking for a moment.*) Yes, it is, isn't it?

**Daniel** We forget. What are we going to do?

**Beth** About what?

**Daniel** You.

**Beth** *walks up the sand to the high-tide line. She sits down.*

**Daniel** *follows her. He sits down.*

I wish you'd go to the hospital. And at least see them. Give
yourself a chance to decline the treatment.

**Beth** No, my love.

**Daniel** I don't know. What am I to do with you? Stubborn as a
mule.

**Mimiko** *enters. He stops.*

**Mimiko** Clare says, I have to come and tell you, she won't be
happy until you come and fish with us.

**Beth** It is really way past her bedtime.

**Mimiko** She says it's only nine o'clock. Silly billy.

**Beth** We've got to get her to Athens and on a 'plane tomorrow.

**Mimiko** You will keep putting her in bed an hour before her time. Even her Dad doesn't do that.

**Daniel** It's because we're old.

**Mimiko** I'll tell Clare you're coming. Don't forget about the fish.

**Mimiko** *goes.*

**Beth** You go. I'm going to sit up here. You know what Mimiko's like, he'll be there all night.

**Daniel** Let them, it doesn't matter.

**Beth** (*smiling*) Go on, go. You don't need me there.

**Daniel** (*smiling*) In a minute.

*A pause.*

Will you be all right?

**Beth** I'm fine, Pet.

*A slight pause.*
**Daniel** *stands up.*

**Daniel** The old bones are creaking a bit.

*He looks at* **Beth**.

**Beth** (*smiling*) Go on, for goodness sake.

**Daniel** *goes towards* **Mimiko** *and* **Clare**.

**Beth** *is looking at the sea. She stands up, walks to the fire, and turns the fish over.*

*The moonlight fades to blackout.*